One World, One Seed

One World, One Seed

Making the World Great

Dr. A. Romani

AUTHORED
PAGES

Authored Pages | Mt. Prospect, Il USA

(888) 821-3271 | AuthoredPages.com

One World, One Seed: Making the World Great

ISBN: 978-1-970666-00-7 (print, paperback PB)

ISBN: 978-1-970666-01-4 (EPUB)

Library of Congress Control Number: 2025924410

BISAC: OCC019000 | PHI005000 | SEL027000

DEDICATION

To the quiet architects of kindness, the steadfast builders of understanding, and the unwavering believers in the power of a gentle hand. This collection of stories is a tribute to the countless individuals whose daily actions, often unseen and unheralded, weave the very fabric of a more compassionate world. And to every reader who seeks to find the extraordinary within the ordinary, may these narratives ignite a spark within your heart, reminding you of the profound impact that you, too, can have.

PREFACE

In a world often characterized by its clamor and complexity, where the grand gestures frequently overshadow the subtle yet significant, this book embarks on a journey to illuminate the profound influence of simple, intentional acts. We are a species bound by an intricate web of interconnectedness, a global family navigating the shared currents of existence. Within this shared space, the seeds of a better world are sown not through monumental feats, but through the consistent cultivation of kindness, the quiet practice of respect, and the deep-seated honor we extend to one another. This collection explores how these fundamental human qualities, when woven into the tapestry of our daily lives, possess the remarkable power to transform not only our individual experiences but also the collective landscape we inhabit. It is a testament to the belief that contentment, found not in the pursuit of excessive material accumulation but in living mindfully and within our means, is a cornerstone of personal well-being and a catalyst for societal harmony. Through these narratives, we aim to inspire a renewed appreciation for the quiet strength of character and the enduring impact of living a life grounded in empathy, financial prudence, and a real deep respect for the human spirit.

TABLE OF CONTENTS

INTRODUCTION

The pursuit of a more beautiful world, a world steeped in peace and illuminated by love, is a quest that resides within the heart of humanity. It is a journey that often feels daunting, a monumental endeavor that can leave us questioning the impact of our individual efforts. Yet, the truth, as these stories aim to reveal, lies not in the scale of our actions, but in the sincerity of our intent and the consistency of our practice. We are all contributors to the grand narrative of human existence, each playing a role, however seemingly small, in shaping the collective experience. This collection of stories serves as a gentle exploration into the profound power that lies within each of us to foster positive change. It delves into the quiet revolutions that begin with a simple act of kindness, the sturdy foundations laid by genuine respect, and the enduring strength found in honoring one another. We are, after all, one global family, bound by shared aspirations and a common destiny.

By embracing financial prudence—the wisdom of living within our means—we unlock a deeper sense of personal freedom and well-being, freeing ourselves from the anxieties of debt and the endless pursuit of more. This contentment, born from mindful stewardship of our resources, ripples outward, contributing to a more stable and harmonious society. The narratives presented herein are not merely tales; they are invitations. Invitations to recognize the interconnectedness of all beings, to celebrate the quiet heroism of everyday decency, and to understand that true greatness is not measured by material possessions, but by the depth of our compassion and the breadth of our empathy. May these stories inspire you to find the extraordinary within the ordinary, and to embrace the power you hold to make the world a kinder, more respectful, and ultimately, a more loving place for all.

DESCRIPTION

Picture a world where empathy moves beyond sympathy—where compassion flourishes as action, and mutual respect is the cornerstone of society. This collection does more than inspire; it challenges you to embrace a holistic vision of greatness defined by love and kindness rather than material wealth. By nurturing your inner joy and practicing mindful living, you open the door to sustainable happiness that brightens not just your days but the legacy you leave for generations to come. *Are you ready to become a part of a greater story—a global family united by shared aspirations and a common destiny?* Embrace these gentle revolutions and see how your sincere intentions and consistent efforts can shape the world in beautiful, lasting ways. This is your invitation to transform the ordinary into the extraordinary and weave a future rooted in peace, respect, and love.

Chapter 1: The Ripple Effect of a Single Kind Act

The Power of a Gentle Word

In the grand tapestry of human interaction, where grand gestures often steal the spotlight, the quiet power of a gentle word can be easily overlooked. Yet, it is within these seemingly small utterances—a genuine compliment, a word of encouragement, a simple expression of gratitude—that a profound and often underestimated force resides. These verbal affirmations, offered with sincerity, possess the remarkable ability to shift the course of an individual's day, to mend fractured spirits, and even to alter the trajectory of a life. They are the invisible threads that weave the fabric of our relationships, strengthening the bonds that connect us within families, workplaces, and communities.

Consider the impact of a simple "You did a great job on that presentation." For the person receiving it, this phrase, delivered with a nod of genuine appreciation, can transform a morning of self-doubt into one of confidence. It validates their effort, acknowledges their contribution, and fuels their motivation. This isn't merely about making someone feel good in the moment; it's about planting a seed of belief that can blossom into sustained effort and greater achievement. The cost of uttering such a phrase is virtually nil, a mere expenditure of breath and intention.

Yet, the return on this investment in human connection is immeasurable. It's the start of building trust, fostering a sense of belonging, and creating an environment where individuals feel seen, heard, and valued.

Think about a time you were feeling overwhelmed, perhaps wrestling with a challenging project or facing a personal setback. In such moments, a supportive word from a friend, colleague, or even a stranger can feel like a lifeline. It's a reminder that you are not alone in your struggle, that your efforts are recognized, and that there is hope for overcoming the obstacle. These moments of verbal affirmation aren't always dramatic; they often manifest as quiet acknowledgments during everyday conversations. A teacher remarking on a student's persistent effort, even if the outcome wasn't perfect, can instill a resilience that serves that student long after they leave the classroom. A manager who notices and praises a team member's meticulous attention to detail, a quality easily missed in the rush of deadlines, can foster a deeper commitment to excellence and a stronger sense of loyalty.

The power of a gentle word lies in its accessibility. It requires no special skills, no significant resources, only a conscious decision to offer kindness. It is a form of giving that is available to everyone, at any time, in any situation. We often underestimate our capacity to influence others through our words, perhaps because the impact isn't always immediately visible or quantifiable. However, the cumulative effect of these small acts of verbal affirmation can be transformative. They create a positive feedback loop, where encouragement breeds further effort, appreciation fosters loyalty, and genuine praise cultivates confidence.

Let's explore a scenario. Imagine a young professional, Sarah, who is new to a demanding industry. She's working long hours, feeling the pressure to prove herself, and often second-guessing her abilities. One afternoon, after a particularly challenging meeting where she felt her contributions were overlooked, her direct supervisor, Mr. Harrison, approaches her desk. Instead of moving on to the next urgent task, he pauses. "Sarah," he says, his tone warm and sincere, "I wanted to acknowledge your insightful question during the client discussion this morning. It really helped clarify a key point for everyone, and I appreciate your courage in asking it when others were hesitant." This simple acknowledgment, delivered privately and genuinely, lands on Sarah like a much-needed ray of sunshine. It cuts through her self-doubt, validates her effort, and reinforces her decision to be bold. The rest of her day feels lighter, her motivation renewed. She leaves the office that evening with a spring in her step, feeling a renewed sense of purpose and belonging. This one gentle word, offered without expectation of immediate return, has likely altered the course of her day, boosted her confidence, and strengthened her resolve to persevere in her career.

Consider another instance within a family setting. A parent is diligently helping their child with homework, a task that has become a nightly ritual, often fraught with frustration for both. The child, Leo, is struggling with a math concept, his brow furrowed in concentration. The parent, tired from a long day, feels the urge to rush through the process. Instead, they take a deep breath and say, "Leo, I see how hard you're working on this. It's not easy, but you're really sticking with it. I'm proud of your effort." Leo looks up, surprised. He had been feeling discouraged, believing he wasn't smart enough. This simple praise for his effort, rather than focusing solely on the correctness of his answers, shifts his perspective. He realizes that the process of learning is valued, not just the immediate outcome. This fosters a healthier relationship with challenges, a crucial lesson for his academic and personal development. The parent, in turn, experiences a moment of connection and satisfaction, realizing that their gentle words have contributed to their child's resilience and self-esteem in a way that a purely outcome-focused approach might not have.

The ripple effect of these words extends beyond the immediate recipient. When individuals feel appreciated and encouraged, they are more likely to extend that same kindness to others. Sarah, feeling validated by her supervisor, might be more inclined to offer a word of encouragement to a junior colleague struggling with their own tasks. Leo, feeling proud of his effort, might be more patient and supportive when his younger sibling needs help with their own homework. This is the essence of the ripple effect: a single, gentle word, emanating from one person, can touch multiple lives, creating a positive chain reaction that strengthens the entire community.

This phenomenon is not confined to personal relationships; it plays out in professional environments as well. In a team setting, where deadlines are tight and pressures are high, a culture of appreciation can significantly impact morale and productivity. A leader who consistently acknowledges the contributions of their team members, not just in public forums but in everyday interactions, cultivates a more positive and collaborative atmosphere. When team members feel their work is seen and valued, they are more likely to go the extra mile, to support their colleagues, and to approach challenges with a sense of shared purpose. This creates a virtuous cycle where positive reinforcement fuels engagement, and engagement drives better outcomes. The opposite is also true: a lack of verbal acknowledgment can lead to disengagement, resentment, and a decline in overall performance.

The subtle art of delivering a gentle word also involves authenticity. A hollow compliment or insincere praise can be easily detected and can even have a negative effect, breeding cynicism rather than warmth. The power lies in the genuine intention behind the words. It's about noticing the small things, recognizing the effort, and speaking from a place of sincerity. This requires us to be present in our interactions, to truly see and hear the people around us, and to consciously choose words that uplift and affirm.

Consider the impact of a simple "Thank you for holding the door" from a stranger as you navigate a busy street, laden with packages. It's a fleeting moment, but it acknowledges your presence and your minor effort, making you feel seen and appreciated in the anonymity of the crowd. Or the barista who, with a warm smile, says, "Have a wonderful day!" as they hand you your coffee. These small, genuine gestures, fueled by gentle words, create momentary pockets of positivity in our otherwise busy lives. They remind us of our shared humanity and the simple joy of human connection.

Furthermore, the impact of a gentle word can be particularly profound for those who are struggling or feeling isolated. In times of grief, illness, or personal hardship, a few carefully chosen words of comfort and support can make a world of difference. "I'm so sorry for your loss," or "I'm thinking of you," or "I'm here if you need anything," are not cures for pain, but they are powerful expressions of solidarity and care. They communicate that someone is bearing witness to another's suffering and offering solace. This empathetic acknowledgment can provide strength and comfort during the darkest of times, reminding individuals that they are not alone in their journey.

The economic argument for kindness is often overlooked. While we frequently focus on financial investments and material gains, the "return on investment" for acts of kindness, particularly through words, is deeply rooted in human connection and well-being. When we create environments where people feel valued and supported through gentle words, we foster loyalty, reduce employee turnover, improve customer satisfaction, and build stronger community ties. These are all tangible benefits that contribute to a more stable and prosperous society. A workplace where genuine appreciation is a regular currency is likely to be more innovative, more resilient, and ultimately, more successful. Similarly, a community where neighbors offer words of support and encouragement is likely to be more cohesive and better equipped to face collective challenges.

The accessibility of this form of giving is also what makes it so powerful. It doesn't require extensive training or significant financial resources. It is an innate human capacity that we can choose to cultivate and employ daily. It's about shifting our mindset from one of scarcity to one of abundance, recognizing that we have a wealth of positive words to share. It's about being intentional in our interactions, choosing to focus on the good in others and expressing that recognition verbally.

The impact of a gentle word is also amplified when it is shared within families. Parents who regularly offer words of affirmation and encouragement to their children are nurturing their self-esteem and building a foundation of unconditional love. Children who hear "I love you," "I'm proud of you," and "You can do it," are more likely to develop a strong sense of self-worth and resilience. These words create a secure emotional base from which they can explore the world and face challenges. Similarly, in adult relationships, expressing appreciation and offering words of support can strengthen marital bonds, deepen friendships, and foster a sense of partnership and mutual respect. A simple "Thank you for listening" after a difficult conversation, or "I appreciate your support with this," can go a long way in reinforcing connection and understanding.

Moreover, this practice extends to how we interact with service providers. Acknowledging the efforts of a cashier, a waiter, a delivery driver, or a customer service representative with a genuine "Thank you" or "I appreciate your help" can make a significant difference in their day. These individuals often perform tasks that can be demanding and overlooked, and a simple word of recognition can humanize the interaction and offer a moment of genuine connection. It's a reminder that behind every service rendered is a person who deserves to be treated with dignity and respect.

The psychological underpinnings of this phenomenon are well-documented. Positive psychology research consistently highlights the benefits of gratitude, positive affirmations, and social support on mental and emotional well-being. When we offer these things to others through our words, we are not only uplifting them but also activating the same positive neural pathways within ourselves. The act of giving kindness, even in the form of a gentle word, releases endorphins, reduces stress hormones, and fosters a sense of purpose and connection.

In essence, the power of a gentle word is the power of human connection amplified. It is the recognition that our words have weight, that they can build up or tear down, inspire or discourage. By consciously choosing to use our words to affirm, encourage, and appreciate, we become agents of positive change in the lives of those around us. We contribute to creating environments where individuals feel safe to be themselves, where efforts are recognized, and where connection thrives. This subtle yet potent force, available to us all, is one of the most accessible and impactful ways to weave a more positive and supportive tapestry in our families, our communities, and ultimately, in the world. It's a reminder that while grand gestures may capture attention, it is often the quiet, consistent power of a gentle word that truly transforms lives.

The profound impact of a single compliment or word of encouragement, delivered genuinely, can alter an individual's trajectory for the day, or even longer. This isn't just about fleeting positivity; it's about fundamental human connection. Think about the last time someone genuinely praised your effort on a task. It might have been a colleague noticing your meticulous research, a friend appreciating your thoughtful advice, or a family member acknowledging your patience. How did that feel? For many, such moments provide a vital boost of confidence, a validation of their hard work, and a renewed sense of purpose. This small verbal affirmation can act as a powerful antidote to self-doubt, transforming a potentially disheartening experience into an opportunity for growth and resilience. It's akin to receiving a much-needed energy boost, fueling motivation and encouraging continued effort.

We will examine real-world scenarios where supportive dialogue fostered resilience and opened doors to unforeseen opportunities. Consider the student who, after receiving encouraging feedback from a teacher on a challenging assignment, feels inspired to pursue further study in that subject, eventually leading to a fulfilling career. Or the entrepreneur who, on the brink of giving up due to numerous setbacks, receives a word of belief from a mentor or investor, reigniting their passion and driving them to persevere, ultimately leading to success. These are not isolated incidents; they are testaments to the tangible outcomes of empathetic and encouraging communication. The cost of these words is negligible—a few moments of attention, a conscious choice of phrasing—but their return on investment in human connection is immeasurable. They build trust, foster a sense of belonging, and create environments where individuals feel safe to take risks and express themselves authentically.

The focus remains on the personal, accessible nature of this form of giving, highlighting its role in strengthening interpersonal bonds within families and communities. Unlike material gifts or grand gestures, words of encouragement and appreciation require no financial outlay. They are a readily available resource that everyone possesses. This accessibility democratizes the act of giving, making it possible for anyone, regardless of their economic circumstances, to make a significant positive impact on others. In families, consistently offering words of affirmation to children—"I'm proud of you," "You're doing a great job," "I love you"—builds a strong foundation of self-esteem and emotional security. These words act as emotional anchors, helping children navigate the complexities of life with greater confidence. In communities, a simple "Thank you" to a volunteer, a word of encouragement to a neighbor facing a difficulty, or a sincere compliment to a local business owner can foster a stronger sense of unity and mutual support. These small acts, when woven together, create a powerful social fabric that enhances overall well-being.

Let's delve deeper into specific examples. Imagine a busy parent juggling work, household responsibilities, and childcare. They might feel unappreciated and exhausted. A simple "Thank you for making dinner tonight, it was delicious," from their partner or child, delivered with sincerity, can completely reframe their perspective. It acknowledges their effort and expresses gratitude, validating their contribution and alleviating some of the perceived burden. This small act of verbal appreciation can shift the emotional climate of the household, fostering a greater sense of teamwork and mutual respect. It's not about expecting constant praise, but about recognizing the cumulative impact of consistent, genuine acknowledgment.

In a professional setting, consider a team working on a demanding project with a tight deadline. One team member, Alex, goes above and beyond, staying late several nights to ensure the project's success. When the project is completed, the team lead, instead of simply moving on to the next task, makes a point of publicly acknowledging Alex's dedication and extra effort. "I want to specifically thank Alex for their incredible commitment to this project. Alex's willingness to put in the extra hours was instrumental in our success, and I deeply appreciate that." This public affirmation not only validates Alex's hard work but also serves as a positive example for the rest of the team, reinforcing the value of dedication and teamwork. It inspires a culture where hard work is recognized and rewarded, not just financially, but through genuine appreciation.

The power of a gentle word is also evident in how it can diffuse tense situations and de-escalate conflict. When disagreements arise, responding with empathy and understanding, rather than defensiveness or aggression, can pave the way for resolution. A phrase like, "I understand you feel frustrated, and I want to hear your perspective," can open the door to a more productive conversation. It signals a willingness to listen and to acknowledge the other person's feelings, even if there isn't immediate agreement. This approach, rooted in respect and empathy, can transform potential confrontation into an opportunity for deeper understanding and stronger relationships.

Furthermore, the impact of words can be amplified when they are used to acknowledge the unseen efforts of others. We often overlook the daily contributions of those who maintain our communities—the sanitation workers, the public transport operators, the childcare providers. A simple "Thank you for your hard work" or "I appreciate you keeping our streets clean" can offer a moment of recognition and validation to individuals whose labor is often taken for granted. These acts of acknowledgment humanize our interactions and foster a greater sense of shared responsibility and appreciation within society.

The ripple effect continues. When individuals consistently experience and offer gentle words of affirmation, they become more attuned to the emotional needs of others. This heightened awareness fosters greater empathy, which in turn leads to more acts of kindness and support. It's a virtuous cycle where positive communication breeds more positive interactions, creating a more compassionate and supportive environment for everyone. The person who receives a word of encouragement is more likely to "pay it forward," extending that same kindness to someone else, thus amplifying the initial act.

Think about a community garden. While the physical act of gardening involves tending plants, the social aspect often involves sharing advice, offering help with a difficult task, or simply a friendly chat. A gardener who has a particularly bountiful harvest might offer a word of advice to a novice gardener struggling with pests, or share some of their produce, accompanied by a simple "I hope this helps." This exchange, fueled by gentle words and a spirit of sharing, strengthens community bonds and fosters a collaborative environment. It's a tangible illustration of how small acts of verbal kindness and support can cultivate a thriving shared space.

In the context of financial well-being, even here, the power of a gentle word plays a role. For instance, when someone is struggling with debt, offering words of support and encouragement without judgment can be incredibly valuable. Phrases like, "It's understandable that you're feeling overwhelmed, but there are resources available to help," or "I believe in your ability to work through this," can provide the emotional fortitude needed to tackle financial challenges. This support system, built on empathetic communication, can be as crucial as practical financial advice in helping individuals regain control of their finances and build a more secure future.

The cumulative effect of these small, consistent acts of verbal kindness can lead to a significant shift in the overall atmosphere of our interactions. It's about creating a culture where empathy is valued, where appreciation is expressed freely, and where encouragement is a common currency.

This doesn't mean avoiding constructive criticism but rather ensuring that it is delivered with respect and a genuine desire for the other person's growth. The intention behind the words, coupled with their delivery, is paramount.

Ultimately, the power of a gentle word underscores a fundamental truth: our words matter. They have the capacity to shape perceptions, build relationships, and influence outcomes in profound ways. By consciously choosing to use our language to uplift, affirm, and encourage, we contribute to a more positive, resilient, and connected world. This accessible, yet immensely powerful, form of giving is a cornerstone of genuine human interaction and a vital ingredient in fostering both individual well-being and the strength of our communities. It is a continuous opportunity for us to practice empathy, to extend kindness, and to weave a richer, more supportive tapestry in our daily lives, one gentle word at a time.

Bridging Divides Through Respect

The intricate tapestry of human existence is woven with threads of countless beliefs, experiences, and viewpoints. In our increasingly interconnected world, encountering perspectives that diverge from our own is not an anomaly but a certainty. Navigating these differences with grace and efficacy hinges on a fundamental quality: respect. This is not a passive acceptance, nor an endorsement of every ideology, but a profound acknowledgment of the inherent worth and dignity of every individual, regardless of their background or the opinions they hold. It is the cornerstone upon which understanding is built and the bridge that spans the chasms of disagreement.

Actively listening is the primary conduit through which respect flows. It is an engaged process, far removed from simply waiting for one's turn to speak. True listening involves suspending judgment, setting aside preconceived notions, and making a conscious effort to comprehend the speaker's message, both its explicit content and its underlying emotional currents. When we truly listen, we signal to the other person that their voice is valued, that their perspective is worthy of consideration. This act of validation can disarm defensiveness and open the door to genuine dialogue. Consider the myriads of global forums and peace negotiations throughout history. While agreements were often the ultimate goal, the foundational step, without which no progress could be made, was the mutual willingness of opposing parties to listen to one another, even when those words were difficult to hear. This listening, often initiated with a commitment to hear, not necessarily to agree, creates a psychological space where empathy can begin to take root.

It is in this space that the possibility of finding common ground, however small, emerges.

Valuing differing opinions, even when they fundamentally challenge our own deeply held beliefs, is perhaps one of the most demanding yet crucial aspects of cultivating respect. It requires us to recognize that our personal worldview, while valid for us, is not universally absolute. The diversity of human experience naturally leads to a diversity of thought. When we encounter an opinion that clashes with our own, our immediate inclination might be to dismiss it, to argue against it, or to feel personally affronted. However, true respect invites us to pause. It encourages us to ask: "What experiences, what information, what reasoning has led this person to this conclusion?" This is not about adopting their viewpoint, but about understanding the genesis of it. This intellectual curiosity, driven by respect, can lead to profound personal growth. It sharpens our own arguments by forcing us to articulate them more clearly and to consider their limitations.

History offers numerous examples of how societies have either thrived or faltered based on their approach to diversity of thought. In the ancient Athenian democracy, for instance, citizens were encouraged to engage in public discourse and debate. While not always harmonious, the very structure of their political life was built on the premise that diverse voices, even dissenting ones, contributed to the collective good and informed decision-making. Philosophers like Socrates, who constantly questioned established norms, thrived in this environment, pushing the boundaries of understanding through respectful, albeit persistent, inquiry. Conversely, societies that have suppressed dissent, that have enforced ideological uniformity, have often stagnated and become brittle. The forced conformity eliminates the friction necessary for intellectual innovation and adaptation, ultimately weakening the social fabric.

In a more contemporary context, consider the advancements spurred by collaborative efforts across disciplines and cultures. Scientific breakthroughs, for example, rarely emerge from a single, isolated mind working within a vacuum of like-minded individuals. Instead, they are often the product of diverse teams, bringing together physicists, biologists, engineers, ethicists, and sociologists, each contributing a unique perspective. A groundbreaking medical treatment, for instance, might stem from the insight of a researcher who, through rigorous experimentation, challenges existing paradigms, but its development and ethical implementation require input from a much broader spectrum of expertise. This cross-pollination of ideas, fueled by a mutual respect for each other's specialized knowledge and a shared commitment to a common goal, is essential for progress. When individuals within these teams feel their contributions are respected, even if their specific ideas are not ultimately adopted, they are more likely to remain engaged and contribute to the collective effort.

The principle of respecting inherent dignity is paramount. This means recognizing that every human being possesses intrinsic value, a worth that is not contingent upon their agreement with us, their accomplishments, or their social standing. It is about seeing the humanity in the other, even when their beliefs or actions are difficult to comprehend or condone. This is a challenging concept, particularly when confronted with actions that may seem abhorrent. Yet, the capacity for respect is not meant to equate to condoning harmful behavior. Rather, it is the recognition that even within individuals who perpetrate harm, there is a human being whose inherent dignity, however violated, remains. This is a distinction that allows for accountability and justice while preserving the fundamental humanistic principle. When we lose sight of this inherent dignity, our responses can descend into dehumanization, a dangerous path that often perpetuates cycles of conflict and suffering.

Building bridges through respect requires conscious effort. It involves actively seeking commonalities, identifying shared aspirations, and framing discussions in ways that emphasize mutual benefit. Instead of focusing solely on points of contention, we can pivot towards areas of agreement, however minor. For instance, in a workplace dispute between departments with differing priorities, a leader might facilitate a discussion by first acknowledging the shared organizational goal—success, customer satisfaction, or innovation. By framing the resolution of their conflict as a means to achieve this common objective, the leader fosters an environment where respect for each other's roles and contributions becomes more natural. This approach helps to shift the narrative from "us versus them" to "us working together for a common purpose."

The global migration patterns of the 21st century present a powerful, real-world laboratory for observing the impact of respect on societal cohesion. As people from diverse cultural, religious, and socio-economic backgrounds increasingly interact within single communities, the ability to navigate these differences with respect becomes critical. Communities that embrace newcomers with a genuine desire to understand their cultures, to learn from their experiences, and to offer them opportunities to contribute, tend to experience greater social harmony and economic vitality. Conversely, communities that react with suspicion, fear, and intolerance, often erect barriers that lead to social fragmentation, economic underperformance, and increased conflict. The former approach, rooted in respect, fosters integration and mutual enrichment; the latter, born from a lack of it, breeds alienation and division.

Consider the historical narratives of religious tolerance and intolerance. Periods of significant societal advancement have often coincided with eras where different religious groups, despite theological differences, coexisted with mutual respect, allowing for cultural and intellectual exchange. For example, in parts of the medieval Islamic world, scholars and communities of various faiths often interacted, sharing knowledge and contributing to a vibrant intellectual milieu. This flourishing was underpinned by a degree of mutual respect that allowed for peaceful coexistence and collaboration. In stark contrast, periods of religious persecution and enforced conversion have historically led to immense suffering, social instability, and the suppression of knowledge and innovation. These historical accounts serve as stark reminders that respect for differing beliefs is not merely a matter of politeness but a fundamental requirement for peaceful and progressive societies.

The digital age has amplified both the opportunities for connection and the challenges of misunderstanding. Online platforms, while offering unprecedented access to diverse voices, can also become echo chambers for prejudice and division if not navigated with care. The anonymity offered by some online spaces can embolden individuals to express disrespect and animosity that they might not in face-to-face interactions. Here, the practice of extending respect becomes even more vital. It means being mindful of the impact of our words in virtual spaces, choosing to engage with empathy, and resisting the urge to participate in online vitriol. It also means actively seeking out diverse perspectives online and engaging with them constructively, rather than retreating into curated content that merely reinforces existing beliefs. The ability to engage respectfully with those who hold opposing views in online forums can be a powerful force for bridging divides and fostering understanding in the digital sphere, demonstrating that respect is not limited to physical proximity.

The concept of respect also extends to how we approach disagreements over resources or political ideologies. When competing interests arise, a respectful approach involves acknowledging the legitimacy of differing needs and perspectives, rather than immediately resorting to adversarial tactics. For instance, in resource management conflicts, such as water rights disputes between agricultural and urban communities, a respectful dialogue would involve understanding the essential role water plays for each group. It would mean listening to their concerns, acknowledging their dependence on the resource, and collaboratively seeking solutions that, while perhaps requiring compromise, are perceived as fair and equitable by all parties. This process, underpinned by mutual respect, is far more likely to yield sustainable and socially acceptable outcomes than a purely power-based or confrontational approach.

Furthermore, personal relationships are profoundly shaped by the presence or absence of respect. Within families, for example, respecting the autonomy and individual journey of each member, even as they navigate life choices that differ from parental expectations, is crucial for maintaining healthy bonds. A parent who respects their adult child's career path, even if it deviates from their own aspirations, or their choice of partner, even if it surprises them, fosters an environment of trust and open communication. This respect allows the relationship to evolve and adapt, preventing resentment and estrangement. It's about valuing the person over the projection of one's own desires.

In the professional sphere, respect for colleagues' contributions, expertise, and personal boundaries is foundational for effective teamwork and a positive work environment. When individuals feel their efforts are recognized and their opinions are considered, they are more likely to be engaged, productive, and loyal. Conversely, a workplace characterized by a lack of respect—through dismissive comments, demeaning behavior, or the appropriation of ideas—can lead to low morale, high turnover, and a decline in overall performance. Building a culture of respect requires consistent effort from leadership and all team members, fostering an environment where everyone feels valued and empowered.

The financial prudence advocated throughout this book also intersects with respect. Living within one's means is an act of self-respect; it is acknowledging one's limitations and responsibilities and acting with integrity. It means respecting one's financial future and the well-being of oneself and one's dependents. Moreover, financial generosity, when exercised thoughtfully and respectfully, can be a powerful tool for building community and showing solidarity. It is not simply about the act of giving money, but about the spirit in which it is offered—with dignity, without condescension, and with a genuine desire to support another's well-being. This mindful approach to financial interactions reflects a broader respect for the interconnectedness of individuals and their economic circumstances.

Ultimately, the practice of respect is a continuous journey, not a destination. It requires ongoing vigilance, a willingness to learn, and a commitment to understanding. It is the recognition that every person we encounter, regardless of their background or beliefs, is part of our shared human family. By actively listening, valuing diverse opinions, and acknowledging inherent dignity, we dismantle the barriers that divide us and build the bridges that connect us. This commitment to mutual respect is not only a moral imperative but a practical necessity for fostering a more peaceful, collaborative, and flourishing global society. It is in this spirit of profound respect that the ripple effect of a single kind act can truly expand, transforming individuals, communities, and the world at large. The quiet power of respecting another's perspective, even in disagreement, can initiate a cascade of understanding, paving the way for solutions that benefit us all and reinforcing our shared humanity. This deliberate cultivation of respect is, in essence, an investment in a more harmonious and unified future for everyone.

Honoring the Unseen Efforts

The silent hum of progress, the smooth functioning of our daily lives, the very fabric of our communities – these are not mere accidents of existence. They are the meticulously crafted outcomes of countless efforts, many of which remain unseen, unheralded, and often, unacknowledged. In our rush to achieve, to advance, and to build, we sometimes become so focused on the grand vision, the ultimate success, that we overlook the quiet, persistent work of those who laid the groundwork, who kept the machinery turning, who offered a helping hand when it was most needed. This subsection is dedicated to those efforts, the ones that operate below the radar of public acclaim but are nonetheless vital to our collective well-being and the positive ripple effect we aim to create.

Consider the individual who meticulously sorts the recycling, ensuring that valuable materials are diverted from landfills. This is a task often performed without fanfare, perhaps in the early morning or late evening, a solitary act of environmental stewardship. Yet, this quiet commitment contributes to a healthier planet, a cleaner future, and a more sustainable way of living for everyone. Their diligence, their willingness to perform this often-mundane chore, is a testament to a deeper understanding of our interconnectedness with the natural world. It's a personal commitment that has broader implications, a silent contribution to a shared responsibility.

Think also of the administrative assistant who manages schedules, organizes files, and ensures that communication flows smoothly within an office. Their work is the invisible scaffolding that supports the visible achievements of others. Without their organizational prowess, projects would falter, deadlines would be missed, and the entire team's productivity would suffer. They are the orchestrators of efficiency, the unsung heroes who create the conditions for success, often through tasks that are easily taken for granted. Acknowledging their contribution is not just about recognizing their role; it's about understanding how essential their diligent, often unseen, efforts are to the collective output.

The same principle applies within the domestic sphere. The parent who wakes early to prepare lunches, who patiently listens to a child's anxieties, who ensures the household runs smoothly – these are acts of love and dedication that form the bedrock of family life. These contributions, while deeply felt by those who receive them, are often viewed as simply part of a parent's duty, rather than recognized for the immense energy, emotional labor, and unwavering commitment they require. Acknowledging this unseen work fosters a deeper sense of appreciation within the family unit, reinforcing bonds and creating a more supportive and loving environment. It shifts the dynamic from expectation to gratitude.

Even in seemingly transactional relationships, such as those with service providers, there is an opportunity to honor unseen efforts. The barista who remembers your usual order, the cleaner who ensures a public space is welcoming, the delivery driver who braves inclement weather to bring essential goods – these are individuals whose daily efforts contribute to our comfort and convenience. A simple word of thanks, a moment of eye contact and genuine appreciation, can illuminate their day and affirm the value of their work. These small gestures of recognition are like tiny seeds of kindness, planting themselves in the recipient's consciousness and potentially inspiring them to extend similar gestures to others.

The psychological impact of recognition is profound. When our efforts are seen and valued, it validates our work, boosting our sense of self-worth and motivation. This is not about seeking external validation as a primary goal, but rather about the human need to feel that our contributions matter. For individuals who have historically been marginalized or whose work is often devalued, receiving recognition can be particularly powerful. It can serve as an antidote to feelings of invisibility and a confirmation of their inherent value. This psychological boost can translate into increased engagement, greater creativity, and a renewed commitment to one's tasks.

In team settings, the conscious practice of acknowledging unseen efforts can transform group dynamics. When team members actively look for opportunities to appreciate each other's contributions, it fosters a culture of psychological safety and mutual respect. This, in turn, encourages greater collaboration and a willingness to take risks, knowing that their efforts will be seen and valued, regardless of the ultimate outcome. Imagine a project team where one member quietly handles all the data analysis, ensuring accuracy and clarity, while another focuses on client presentations. If the presenter takes credit without acknowledging the foundational work of the analyst, it can breed resentment and stifle future collaboration. However, if the presenter publicly credits the analyst for their meticulous work, it not only uplifts the analyst but also strengthens the team's cohesion and signals to everyone that thoroughness and diligence are prized.

This practice also enriches the giver. The act of consciously looking for the good in others, of seeking out opportunities to offer appreciation, shifts our own focus away from scarcity and towards abundance. It cultivates a more positive and optimistic outlook, enhancing our own sense of well-being. When we make it a habit to acknowledge the efforts of those around us, we become more attuned to the positive aspects of our environment and the contributions of the people within it. This can lead to a deeper sense of connection and belonging, strengthening our social bonds and fostering a more supportive and fulfilling life. It's a powerful reminder that kindness is a two-way street, its benefits rippling outwards to touch both the giver and the receiver.

Consider the impact on customer service. A restaurant server who goes the extra mile to accommodate a dietary restriction, a retail associate who patiently helps a customer find the perfect item, a customer support agent who remains calm and helpful during a difficult call – these are all examples of individuals performing their duties with a level of care and dedication that transcends the minimum expectation. When patrons or managers take the time to acknowledge these efforts, whether through a compliment, a positive review, or a direct word of thanks, it not only validates the employee's hard work but also reinforces the business's commitment to excellent service. This positive reinforcement can inspire others to emulate that dedication, creating a virtuous cycle of appreciation and high-quality service.

The narrative of financial prudence, so central to our journey towards contentment, also finds a powerful ally in the practice of honoring unseen efforts. When we live within our means, we often rely on the efforts of others in ways we may not always fully appreciate. The farmer who grows our food, the construction worker who built our homes, the educators who shaped our minds – these are all essential contributors to our quality of life, whose labor, often physically demanding and underappreciated, underpins our very existence. By living responsibly and not burdening others with our financial irresponsibility, we, in a sense, honor their efforts by not contributing to a system that might exploit them. Furthermore, when we are in a position to offer financial support or assistance, doing so with a deep respect for the dignity and efforts of the recipient transforms the act from mere charity into a meaningful gesture of solidarity and shared humanity. It acknowledges their inherent worth and the value of their contributions, seen or unseen.

In educational settings, the impact of recognizing unseen efforts is equally profound. Teachers often pour immense personal time and energy into lesson planning, grading, and providing individual support to students. Many students, however, only see the final product – the lesson delivered, the grade received. When students make an effort to acknowledge the behind-the-scenes work of their educators, perhaps through a heartfelt note or a word of thanks at the end of the semester, it can be incredibly validating. Similarly, in academic research, the tireless work of lab technicians, research assistants, and archivists is often crucial to groundbreaking discoveries but rarely receives the public spotlight. Publicly acknowledging these vital contributions not only gives credit where it is due but also highlights the collaborative nature of progress and inspires future generations to value all forms of diligent work.

The ripple effect of honoring unseen efforts extends outwards to shape the very culture of our interactions. When we cultivate a habit of gratitude and appreciation, we contribute to a more positive, supportive, and interconnected society. This creates an environment where individuals are more likely to extend kindness to strangers, to support community initiatives, and to engage in acts of civic responsibility. It fosters a sense of shared purpose, reminding us that we are all part of a larger whole, reliant on each other's contributions for our collective flourishing. In essence, by consciously choosing to see and value the often-invisible work that sustains us, we actively participate in building a world where everyone feels recognized, respected, and valued, amplifying the positive impact of every single act of kindness. This deliberate practice of acknowledgment serves as a powerful engine for generating goodwill, fostering stronger relationships, and ultimately, making the world a demonstrably better place for all. It's about recognizing the unseen threads that bind us together, and in doing so, strengthening the entire tapestry of human connection.

The Interconnectedness of Humanity

Our lives are not lived in isolation. Despite the illusion of individual journeys, we are inextricably woven into a vast, intricate tapestry of human experience. This fundamental truth, the interconnectedness of humanity, is the very bedrock upon which the ripple effect of a single kind act is built. Each of us, in our unique existence, is a node in a network that spans the globe, touching countless lives in ways we may never fully comprehend. To truly grasp the power of kindness, we must first acknowledge this profound, shared existence.

Consider the simple act of sharing a meal. It is more than just sustenance; it is a ritual that has bound communities together since time immemorial. When we extend an invitation to share our table, or when we contribute to a communal feast, we are not merely offering food. We are offering belonging, fostering connection, and affirming the shared vulnerability that unites us. This gesture, replicated across cultures and continents, forms the invisible threads that hold our global family together.

The farmer who toiled under the sun to grow the grains, the baker who shaped the dough, the hands that prepared the ingredients – all are part of this intricate chain of human effort that culminates in that shared moment. Our gratitude for that meal is, by extension, an acknowledgment of their contribution, a recognition of our dependence on one another.

The same profound connection can be observed in moments of shared adversity. When natural disasters strike, when communities face famine or conflict, the immediate response often transcends national borders. Aid organizations mobilize, governments offer support, and individuals from distant lands contribute what they can, driven by an innate sense of empathy. This outpouring of compassion is not simply a transactional exchange; it is a visceral recognition of our shared humanity. The tears shed for a stranger's suffering, the donations made to alleviate pain felt thousands of miles away, the volunteer hours offered to rebuild lives – these are all powerful testaments to our inherent capacity for connection. They demonstrate that despite our differences in language, culture, or belief, the core of our shared experience—the desire for safety, for dignity, for well-being—remains remarkably consistent.

Think about the stories that resonate with us most deeply – tales of heroism, sacrifice, and unwavering support. These narratives often highlight individuals who, despite personal risk or inconvenience, reached out to help others, even those they had never met. These are not isolated incidents; they are manifestations of a deeper, often unarticulated, understanding that the welfare of one is intrinsically linked to the welfare of all. When a firefighter rushes into a burning building to save a life, they are not just acting for that individual; they are acting on behalf of a shared value system that places the sanctity of life above personal safety. When a doctor volunteers in a remote village, providing medical care where none exists, they are extending the reach of our collective capacity to heal and to care. These actions, though performed by individuals, echo the sentiment that "we are all in this together."

The digital age, while often criticized for fostering superficial connections, also provides powerful examples of our interconnectedness. A viral video of a selfless act can inspire millions, sparking waves of similar kindness across the globe. A crowdfunding campaign for a medical emergency can quickly gather the necessary funds, demonstrating how collective generosity can overcome immense personal challenges. Social media platforms, when used for positive purposes, can become conduits for empathy, allowing us to witness and participate in the joys and sorrows of others, fostering a sense of global community. The ability to share stories, to offer support, and to witness the impact of kindness in real-time shrinks the world and amplifies our shared human experience. What might have once been a localized act of compassion can now ripple outward, touching lives in every corner of the planet, creating a global chorus of shared values.

This interconnectedness is not a passive state; it is an active force that shapes our realities. Our consumption patterns, for instance, have far-reaching implications. The coffee we drink, the clothes we wear, the technologies we use – all have a story that extends far beyond our immediate point of purchase. The hands that picked the coffee beans, the factory workers who assembled the electronics, the farmers who grew the cotton – these individuals, often unseen and unheard, are part of the chain that brings these products to us. Recognizing this connection calls us to consider the impact of our choices, to advocate for fair labor practices, and to support businesses that prioritize ethical sourcing and sustainability. It transforms us from passive consumers into active participants in a global economy, where our decisions have real consequences for other human beings.

Furthermore, our shared reliance on the planet itself underscores our interconnectedness. The air we breathe, the water we drink, the climate that sustains us – these are all global commons, subject to the collective impact of our actions. Pollution generated in one region can affect weather patterns and air quality thousands of miles away. Deforestation in one part of the world can contribute to climate change that impacts every nation. This realization compels us to act not just for our immediate communities, but for the health of the entire planet, recognizing that our well-being is inextricably linked to the well-being of the natural world and all its inhabitants. The urgency of climate action, for example, is a direct acknowledgment of this shared responsibility, a recognition that our collective future depends on our ability to work together for the common good.

The concept of a "global village," once a futuristic ideal, is now our lived reality. We are connected by technology, by trade, by shared challenges like pandemics and climate change, and by our fundamental human needs and aspirations. This interconnectedness means that a single act of kindness, whether it originates in a bustling metropolis or a remote village, has the potential to resonate far beyond its immediate context. It can inspire others, create alliances, and foster a sense of shared purpose that can address even the most complex global issues. When we understand that we are all part of this vast, interconnected web, the impulse to act with compassion and generosity becomes not just a moral imperative, but a practical necessity for our collective survival and flourishing.

The impact of empathy, in particular, highlights this interconnectedness. When we can step into another's shoes, feel their pain, and understand their perspective, we bridge the divides that separate us. This empathetic leap allows us to see beyond superficial differences and recognize the shared essence of our humanity. It is the engine that drives humanitarian aid, the foundation of restorative justice, and the spark that ignites movements for social change. The stories of individuals who have championed causes for marginalized communities, often drawing strength from shared experiences or a profound sense of identification, are powerful examples of this. They demonstrate that even when faced with immense obstacles, the realization that one is not alone, that there are others who understand and care, can be a transformative force.

Consider the ripple effect of education and knowledge sharing. When a teacher dedicates themselves to imparting wisdom, they are not just educating an individual; they are contributing to the collective intellectual capital of humanity. When researchers collaborate across borders to find cures for diseases or solutions to global problems, they are weaving together the threads of human ingenuity for the benefit of all. Open-source software, free online courses, and the open sharing of scientific data are all modern manifestations of this interconnectedness, demonstrating a commitment to shared progress and collective advancement. These acts of knowledge dissemination and collaborative problem-solving underscore the idea that our greatest achievements often arise from our ability to build upon each other's work, to learn from one another, and to pool our collective intelligence.

Our shared vulnerability is also a powerful unifier. Every human being experiences loss, faces challenges, and grapples with uncertainty. This universal experience of human fragility creates a common ground, a shared understanding that transcends cultural and social barriers. When we offer comfort to someone grieving, when we lend support to a struggling friend, or when we simply offer a listening ear to someone in distress, we are acknowledging this shared vulnerability. These acts of compassion affirm that, despite our individual struggles, we are not alone in our experiences. They create moments of profound connection, reminding us that the strength of our human family lies in our ability to support one another through life's inevitable storms.

The beauty of this interconnectedness lies in its subtlety. It is present in the everyday interactions that often go unnoticed: the polite nod from a stranger, the shared smile with a fellow commuter, the helpful direction given to a lost tourist. These small gestures, seemingly insignificant on their own, collectively contribute to a sense of community and belonging. They are the quiet affirmations of our shared existence, the gentle reminders that we are all part of the same human journey. By consciously engaging in these small acts of connection, we reinforce the bonds that tie us together, creating a more harmonious and supportive global society. Each interaction, no matter how brief, is an opportunity to acknowledge another person's presence and to affirm our shared humanity.

The challenge, then, is to cultivate a conscious awareness of this interconnectedness. It requires us to look beyond our immediate self-interest and to consider the broader implications of our actions. It means recognizing that our well-being is not separate from the well-being of others, and that true prosperity is found in collective flourishing. When we embrace this perspective, every act of kindness, no matter how small, becomes a powerful force for positive change. It becomes a contribution to the collective good, a reinforcement of the bonds that unite us, and a testament to the enduring strength of the human spirit. We are not isolated islands; we are part of a vast, dynamic ocean, and our actions send ripples across its surface, touching shores we may never even see. To truly understand the ripple effect of a single kind act is to understand our fundamental place within this magnificent, interconnected human family. It is to recognize that in lifting others, we inevitably lift ourselves, creating a virtuous cycle of compassion and connection that benefits us all. This awareness transforms our individual actions from mere events into contributions to a larger, shared narrative of human progress and collective well-being.

From Individual Acts to Collective Greatness

The tapestry of human experience, as we've explored, is woven with threads of interconnectedness. We are not solitary stars in a dark universe, but rather part of a vast constellation, each influencing the light of the others. While a single act of kindness can spark a remarkable chain reaction, the true transformative power emerges not from isolated sparks, but from the sustained glow of a community embracing these virtues. This is where individual acts coalesce into a force capable of shaping societies, transforming communities, and ushering in an era of collective greatness. The shift from recognizing the potential of one kind act to actively cultivating a culture of kindness, respect, and honor in our daily lives is the crucial step towards unlocking this profound potential.

When we move beyond contemplating the solitary impact of a benevolent gesture and begin to observe how widespread adoption of such behaviors can sculpt the very fabric of our societies, the scope of our understanding expands dramatically. Consider the profound difference between a single act of charity and a community where generosity is not merely an occasional act of goodwill but an ingrained societal norm. In the latter, the social infrastructure itself begins to shift. Reduced poverty rates are often a direct consequence, not just from the direct aid provided, but from the underlying ethos of mutual support that permeates such communities. When neighbors look out for one another, when businesses integrate ethical practices that benefit the wider community, and when public services are imbued with a spirit of service rather than bureaucracy, the entire societal structure strengthens. This isn't about grand, sweeping pronouncements from on high; it's about the consistent, everyday enactment of empathy and consideration by a critical mass of individuals.

The subtle, yet potent, influence of a community that consistently practices respect and honor can manifest in tangible ways. Social cohesion, that intangible yet vital element that binds people together, flourishes in environments where individuals feel seen, valued, and treated with dignity. When respect is the baseline for interaction, from casual conversations to formal dealings, the propensity for misunderstanding and conflict diminishes. Disagreements are approached with a desire to find common ground rather than to assert dominance. This fosters a climate where diverse perspectives can be shared openly, leading to more robust and inclusive decision-making. Imagine a neighborhood where residents make a conscious effort to acknowledge each other, to offer assistance without being asked, and to resolve minor disputes with patience and understanding. This isn't utopian fantasy; it is the observable outcome of a collective commitment to treating each other with inherent worth. Such environments naturally breed greater trust, making collective action on shared goals far more feasible and effective.

Furthermore, the economic implications of societies built on kindness and respect are often underestimated. While profit motives remain, a culture that values ethical conduct and mutual benefit tends to foster more sustainable and equitable economic growth. Businesses that prioritize fair treatment of employees, responsible sourcing, and community engagement often enjoy greater customer loyalty and a more stable workforce. This isn't just about "doing good"; it's about good business practices that are deeply rooted in respect for all stakeholders. Reduced corruption, increased efficiency in public services due to a spirit of service, and a more productive workforce, all contribute to a more prosperous society for everyone. The cumulative effect of countless individuals making ethically sound choices, driven by a shared commitment to a better society, creates an economic ecosystem that is more resilient and beneficial.

The power of aggregated small acts can be seen in the transformation of public spaces. When individuals take pride in their shared environments, whether it's a park, a street, or a community center, these spaces become vibrant hubs of activity and connection. This ownership stems from a collective sense of responsibility, a tangible expression of honor for the shared resources that benefit everyone. Clean streets, well-maintained parks, and active community centers are not the result of singular, heroic efforts, but rather the outcome of consistent, individual contributions – picking up litter, reporting issues, volunteering time, or simply using these spaces respectfully. This collective stewardship fosters a sense of pride and belonging, further strengthening the social fabric and encouraging more positive interactions.

Consider the realm of education and the development of future generations. When the values of kindness, respect, and honor are not just taught in schools but are visibly practiced by adults in positions of influence and within the wider community, they become deeply ingrained in the consciousness of young people. A child who grows up in an environment where adults model respectful communication, where empathy is encouraged, and where honest effort is honored is far more likely to internalize these values themselves. This creates a virtuous cycle, where each generation, equipped with these fundamental virtues, contributes to an ever-improving societal landscape. The long-term impact of this is immeasurable, shaping a future society that is more compassionate, equitable, and progressive.

The narrative of collective greatness is not built on a foundation of individual virtuosity alone, but on the widespread, consistent application of these virtues. It's about moving from "I should be kind" to "We are a kind community." This transition requires a conscious effort to cultivate these behaviors in our daily interactions. It means choosing empathy when faced with a difficult colleague, extending a helping hand to a neighbor, speaking truthfully and respectfully even when it's challenging, and honoring the contributions of others, no matter how small. Each instance, though seemingly minor, adds to the collective momentum. It's like filling a reservoir drop by drop; eventually, it becomes a powerful source.

The impact of this collective ethos is also evident in the way communities handle challenges and adversity. Societies that have a strong foundation of mutual respect and a history of collective action are often better equipped to navigate crises. Whether it's a natural disaster, an economic downturn, or a public health emergency, the pre-existing bonds of trust and goodwill facilitate a more coordinated and effective response. People are more willing to sacrifice personal convenience for the greater good when they believe in the collective endeavor and trust that others will do the same. This shared resilience, born from a culture of caring and mutual responsibility, is a hallmark of collective greatness.

The challenge, then, lies in recognizing that societal progress is not an abstract concept driven by grand policies alone, but a tangible outcome of the countless individual choices we make every day. The seemingly mundane act of holding a door open for someone, offering a word of encouragement, or taking responsibility for a mistake are all building blocks. When these acts are multiplied across a population, they create an undeniable force for positive change. This is what the essence of moving from individual acts to collective greatness: understanding that our personal commitment to kindness, respect, and honor is not just a personal virtue, but a vital contribution to the well-being and advancement of our shared world.

It's about recognizing that the ideal of a harmonious and prosperous society is not a distant utopia, but a potential reality that we actively construct through our everyday interactions. The consistent practice of these virtues transforms abstract ideals into lived experiences. When respect is the currency of exchange, when honor is a guiding principle, and when kindness is the default setting, communities don't just function; they flourish. They become places where individuals feel safe, supported, and empowered to contribute their best, leading to greater innovation, stronger social bonds, and a palpable sense of shared purpose. This cumulative impact of consistent, intentional positive action by many individuals is the true engine of collective greatness, proving that the most profound societal transformations often begin with the simplest of human gestures, amplified by the power of shared commitment.

Chapter 2: The Foundation of Financial Prudence

Living Within Your Means – A Path to Freedom

Living within your means is more than a financial strategy; it is a declaration of independence. It's a conscious choice to build a life on solid ground, free from the perpetual anxiety that accompanies living beyond one's financial capacity. This isn't about austerity or a life devoid of enjoyment. Instead, it's about cultivating a profound sense of control, enabling you to direct your resources – both money and mental energy – towards what truly matters. When your expenses consistently align with or fall below your income, you create a buffer, a space for breathing room in a world that often feels relentlessly demanding. This alignment is the very bedrock of financial prudence, a fundamental principle that unlocks a potent form of personal freedom.

The journey towards financial freedom begins with a clear and honest assessment of your cash flow. This means understanding precisely where your money comes from and, crucially, where it is going. It involves meticulously tracking every dollar earned and every dollar spent. For many, this is the most revealing, and perhaps initially uncomfortable, part of the process. It's an unvarnished look at your financial habits, stripped of wishful thinking or denial. Tools like budgeting apps, spreadsheets, or even a simple notebook can serve as your financial mirror. The goal is not to judge your past spending, but to gain an objective understanding of your present reality. This data-driven approach removes emotion from the equation and presents a factual landscape of your financial life, highlighting patterns that might otherwise remain hidden. It allows you to see the tangible impact of your purchasing decisions, revealing how small, recurring expenses can accumulate into significant outflows over time.

Once you have a clear picture of your income and expenditures, the next step is to make conscious and deliberate spending decisions. This is where the concept of living within your means truly takes shape. It requires a shift in mindset from reactive spending to proactive planning. Instead of impulsively acquiring goods and services, you begin to prioritize. What are your essential needs? What are your desired wants? And critically, how do these align with your income and your long-term financial goals? This doesn't mean eliminating all wants; rather, it means making intentional choices about which wants you can afford without jeopardizing your financial stability. It's about distinguishing between needs and wants, and ensuring that your discretionary spending is truly discretionary, meaning it doesn't come at the expense of your financial health.

Consider the allure of the latest technological gadgets, the trendy clothing, or the spontaneous vacation. These are all enjoyable aspects of life, but when their acquisition consistently outpaces your income, they become anchors rather than enablers of freedom. "Living within your means" means evaluating these desires against your financial reality. Can you comfortably afford this item or experience without dipping into savings, incurring debt, or compromising your ability to meet your obligations? If the answer is no, then the conscious decision is to postpone, to find a more affordable alternative, or to re-evaluate whether the desire is truly worth the financial strain. This process fosters a sense of discipline, a valuable trait that extends far beyond personal finance into all areas of life.

The impact of living within your means extends beyond simply avoiding debt. It's about building a foundation of security and resilience. When you have a surplus of income, you can build an emergency fund. This fund acts as a vital safety net, protecting you from unexpected events such as job loss, medical emergencies, or major home repairs. Without this buffer, such unforeseen circumstances can quickly spiral into debt, creating a cycle that is incredibly difficult to break. An emergency fund provides peace of mind, knowing that you can weather financial storms without derailing your long-term goals or resorting to high-interest loans. This proactive approach to risk management is a hallmark of financial prudence and a direct consequence of aligning your spending with your income.

Furthermore, living within your means empowers you to pursue your passions and invest in your future. When you aren't burdened by excessive debt payments or the constant pressure to keep up with appearances, you free up resources that can be directed towards personal growth, education, investments, or even starting a business. Imagine having the financial freedom to take a course that could advance your career, to invest in a stock market that could grow your wealth, or to dedicate time to a creative project that brings you joy. These are the opportunities that open up when your financial life is managed responsibly. It's about creating a life where your money serves your aspirations, rather than dictating your limitations.

This control over your personal finances is a powerful form of self-respect. It signifies that you value your own well-being and are taking proactive steps to secure your future. When you consistently make choices that honor your financial commitments and prioritize your long-term stability, you are demonstrating self-discipline and responsibility. This internal validation is incredibly empowering. It's a tangible reminder that you are capable of managing your life effectively and that your financial decisions are a reflection of your commitment to yourself.

This self-respect can ripple outwards, influencing your confidence in other areas of your life and fostering a more positive self-image.

The pursuit of "keeping up with the Joneses" is a particularly insidious trap that leads many away from living within their means. The pressure to acquire the same possessions or maintain a similar lifestyle to peers, friends, or neighbors can be immense, often fueled by social media and pervasive consumer culture. However, this constant comparison is a recipe for financial distress. What you see of others is often a curated highlight reel, not a full picture of their financial realities. Many individuals project an image of affluence while secretly struggling with debt. By focusing on your own financial journey and aligning your spending with your actual income and values, you break free from this detrimental cycle. Your financial path should be your own, designed to meet your unique needs and goals, not to mimic someone else's perceived success.

Living within your means also fosters a greater appreciation for what you already possess. When you are not constantly chasing the next acquisition, you tend to find more contentment and satisfaction in your current circumstances. You learn to make the most of what you have, to maintain and repair items rather than immediately replacing them, and to find joy in experiences rather than material possessions. This mindful consumption cultivates gratitude and reduces the constant urge for more, which is a key component of genuine happiness and financial well-being.

It shifts the focus from external validation through possessions to internal satisfaction through contentment and resourceful living.

The process of aligning expenditures with income requires a commitment to financial literacy. Understanding concepts like interest rates, inflation, and the power of compounding can significantly inform your spending and saving decisions. For instance, understanding how credit card interest can exponentially increase the cost of purchases can be a powerful deterrent against impulse buying. Similarly, grasping the benefits of saving and investing early, even small amounts, can lead to substantial wealth accumulation over time due to the principle of compounding. This knowledge empowers you to make informed choices that actively work in your favor, rather than passively falling victim to financial pitfalls. It transforms your relationship with money from one of apprehension to one of informed confidence.

Furthermore, living within your means is a crucial step towards achieving financial independence. Financial independence isn't just about having a lot of money; it's about having enough money that you are no longer dependent on a traditional job to meet your basic needs and desires. By consistently saving and investing a portion of your income, you can build assets that generate passive income over time. This could include dividends from stocks, rental income from properties, or interest from bonds. When this passive income can cover your living expenses, you gain true freedom – the freedom to choose how you spend your time, whether it's pursuing a passion project, spending more time with family, or traveling the world, without the financial constraints that often dictate these choices.

The practical application of living within your means often involves making difficult choices. It might mean opting for a more affordable car, cooking at home more often, finding free or low-cost entertainment options, or delaying certain home renovations. These are not sacrifices in the negative sense, but rather strategic decisions that prioritize your long-term financial health and freedom. Each conscious decision to spend less than you earn is a step towards building a more secure and fulfilling future. It's about recognizing that short-term gratification can sometimes lead to long-term regret, while disciplined financial choices can lead to lasting peace of mind and opportunity.

The empowerment that comes from living within your means is profound. It transforms you from a passive consumer, buffeted by marketing messages and societal expectations, into an active architect of your financial life. You are no longer a slave to your bills or a victim of your financial circumstances. Instead, you are in the driver's seat, making deliberate choices that align with your values and goals. This sense of agency is incredibly liberating and can have a positive impact on your overall mental and emotional well-being. When you feel in control of your finances, you are better equipped to handle stress, make sound decisions in other areas of your life, and enjoy a greater sense of overall life satisfaction. It's a powerful testament to the fact that financial prudence is not about restriction, but about liberation. It's about building a life of purpose and peace, brick by careful financial brick, all grounded in the simple yet transformative act of living within your means. This foundational principle is the gateway to a stable, fulfilling, and truly free financial existence.

The Art of Mindful Spending

The transition from simply "living within your means" to actively practicing "mindful spending" represents a crucial evolution in our relationship with money. It moves beyond the mere arithmetic of income versus expenses and delves into the psychology and philosophy behind our purchasing decisions. Mindful spending is about bringing conscious intention to every financial transaction, transforming the act of spending from a potentially unconscious habit into a deliberate expression of our values and priorities. It's about cultivating a deep awareness of *why* we spend, *what* we spend on, and the ultimate impact of those choices on our lives and our financial well-being.

At its core, mindful spending is the practice of being present and deliberate when engaging with your finances. It's about asking yourself critical questions before, during, and after a purchase.

Why am I buying this? Does it truly serve a need or a genuine want that aligns with my long-term vision for my life? What is the opportunity cost of this purchase – what else could this money be used for? This level of introspection can feel unusual at first, especially for those accustomed to impulsive buying driven by immediate gratification, societal pressures, or simply the ease of modern commerce. However, by consistently engaging in this mindful process, you begin to rewire your spending habits, moving from a reactive state to a proactive and empowered one.

A fundamental pillar of mindful spending is the clear differentiation between needs and wants. Needs are the essential requirements for survival and basic well-being: food, shelter, clothing, healthcare, and essential utilities. Wants, on the other hand, are desires that enhance our lives but are not strictly necessary for survival. These can range from a cup of specialty coffee each morning to the latest smartphone, a vacation, or designer clothing. The line between needs and wants can sometimes blur, and that's where mindfulness becomes critical. For instance, while transportation is a need, a luxury car might be a want. Nutritious food is a need, but gourmet meals every night could be considered a want. Mindful spending requires an honest assessment of which category a particular expenditure falls into for you, in your current circumstances, and in alignment with your goals.

Consider the common practice of daily coffee purchases. For many, that morning cup is a cherished ritual, a small pleasure that brightens their day. If your budget allows and it genuinely contributes to your well-being without derailing your financial goals, it might be classified as a "want" that you consciously choose to prioritize. However, if those daily purchases are straining your budget, preventing you from saving for a down payment on a house, or forcing you to forgo other important expenses, then mindfulness might prompt a re-evaluation. Could you make coffee at home more often? Could you enjoy that special coffee less frequently, perhaps as an occasional treat? The goal isn't necessarily to eliminate all wants, but to ensure that the wants you indulge in are deliberate choices, made with full awareness of their financial implications, rather than unconscious habits.

This conscious evaluation extends to virtually every aspect of spending. When considering a new piece of clothing, mindful spending prompts questions beyond "Do I like this?" It asks: "Do I need this? Do I already own something similar that serves the same purpose? Will this purchase genuinely add value to my wardrobe, or is it an impulse buy driven by a sale or a fleeting trend? How often will I realistically wear it? Does it align with my personal style and values?" By asking these questions, you can significantly reduce the accumulation of "wardrobe orphans" – items that were bought with enthusiasm but rarely worn, representing wasted money and resources.

The pervasive influence of consumer culture and advertising makes mindful spending a constant practice of vigilance. We are bombarded daily with messages designed to create desire and foster a sense of inadequacy if we don't possess the latest products or services. Social media, in particular, often presents highly curated versions of reality, showcasing aspirational lifestyles that can easily trigger comparison and the urge to spend. Mindful spending acts as an antidote to this external pressure. It involves recognizing that what you see online or in advertisements is often a carefully constructed facade, not a reflection of true happiness or financial stability. By focusing on your own values and goals, you build resilience against the constant barrage of marketing.

One powerful technique for cultivating mindful spending is the "pause." Before making any non-essential purchase, especially those that are outside your typical budget or impulse-driven, implement a waiting period. This could be *24* hours, a week, or even longer, depending on the significance of the purchase. During this pause, reflect on the item. Has the initial urge subsided? Do you still genuinely desire it? Can you find a more affordable alternative? Does it truly align with your financial goals? Often, the desire fades after a period of reflection, revealing the purchase to be an unnecessary impulse rather than a true need or a valuable want. This simple act of pausing can save you a significant amount of money and can even prevent the accumulation of buyer's remorse.

Another aspect of mindful spending is critically evaluating promotional offers and sales. The allure of a "discount" can be incredibly powerful, often leading people to buy things they wouldn't have otherwise considered, simply because they appear to be a good deal. However, a discount on something you don't need is not a saving; it's an unnecessary expense. Mindful shoppers approach sales with a predetermined list and a clear understanding of what they are willing to pay. If an item isn't on your list and doesn't meet your criteria for need or value, the sale price is irrelevant. It's crucial to ask yourself: "Would I buy this at its full price?" If the answer is no, then the sale is likely a trap, not an opportunity.

The practice of mindful spending also involves understanding the emotional triggers behind your purchases. Do you shop when you're stressed, bored, sad, or celebrating? Many purchases are not driven by a rational need but by an attempt to fulfill an emotional void or to boost one's mood. Recognizing these emotional patterns is a vital step in breaking free from compulsive spending. If you find yourself reaching for your wallet when you're feeling down, consider alternative coping mechanisms that don't involve financial expenditure. This might include going for a walk, talking to a friend, engaging in a hobby, or practicing mindfulness meditation. By addressing the underlying emotions directly, you reduce the reliance on spending as a coping mechanism.

Furthermore, mindful spending encourages a shift in focus from acquiring possessions to valuing experiences. Research consistently shows that experiences, such as travel, concerts, learning new skills, or spending time with loved ones, often bring greater and more lasting happiness than material goods. When you prioritize spending on experiences, you create memories and foster personal growth, which are intangible yet incredibly valuable assets. This doesn't mean completely abandoning the purchase of tangible items, but it suggests a rebalancing of priorities. Instead of saving up for the next big gadget, perhaps you save for a weekend getaway, a workshop that sparks your creativity, or a memorable meal with family.

The concept of "value alignment" is also central to mindful spending. This means ensuring that your spending habits reflect your deepest values. If you value sustainability, you might choose to buy from ethically sourced or environmentally friendly brands, even if they are slightly more expensive. If you value community, you might choose to support local businesses. If you value health and well-being, you might invest in high-quality food or fitness activities. When your spending aligns with your values, each purchase becomes an affirmation of what you believe in, adding a layer of purpose and satisfaction to your financial decisions. This creates a more coherent and fulfilling life, where your actions are in harmony with your beliefs.

Tracking your spending, as discussed in the previous sections, is not just about understanding where your money goes, but also about gaining insights into your spending habits and their alignment with your intentions. A mindful spender reviews their expenditure not just for the numbers, but for the story they tell about their priorities. Did I spend more on impulse buys than I intended? Did my spending reflect my stated values of saving for a down payment? Was I mindful in my choices, or did I succumb to external pressures? This regular review process allows for continuous adjustment and refinement of your mindful spending approach.

One practical tool for mindful spending is to categorize your expenses not just by type (e.g., food, housing, entertainment) but also by intention. You might create categories such as "Essential Needs," "Values-Aligned Wants," "Emotional Buys," and "Impulse Purchases." Regularly reviewing these categories can highlight areas where your spending might be unconsciously deviating from your intentions. Seeing a large amount in the "Impulse Purchases" category, for example, can be a powerful motivator to implement stricter pausing strategies or to address underlying emotional triggers.

Ultimately, mindful spending is about cultivating a conscious and intentional relationship with money. It's about recognizing that every dollar spent is a choice, a vote for the kind of life you want to live. By being present, asking critical questions, differentiating between needs and wants, resisting impulse buys, critically evaluating consumer culture, addressing emotional triggers, prioritizing experiences, aligning spending with values, and regularly reviewing your habits, you can transform your financial life. This approach not only leads to greater financial security and freedom but also to a more purposeful, satisfying, and fulfilling existence, where your money truly serves you and your deepest aspirations. It's a journey of self-discovery, empowerment, and conscious creation, turning the mundane act of spending into a powerful tool for living a life well-lived.

Contentment – The True Measurement of Wealth

The relentless pursuit of "more" often forms the bedrock of conventional financial advice. We are conditioned to believe that wealth accumulation is the ultimate goal, a never-ending race to acquire greater assets, higher income, and more possessions. This narrative, deeply ingrained in our societal consciousness, frequently equates financial success with a larger bank account or a more opulent lifestyle. However, this perspective, while seemingly practical on the surface, can inadvertently lead us down a path where the very instruments we use to achieve financial security become sources of perpetual dissatisfaction. The constant striving can overshadow a more profound and accessible form of wealth – contentment.

Contentment is not a passive acceptance of one's circumstances, nor is it an excuse for financial stagnation. Instead, it is an active, cultivated state of mind that acknowledges and appreciates the present, finding a deep sense of satisfaction and sufficiency within it. It is the quiet realization that while progress is valuable, the absence of constant longing for what we do not have is a powerful, often overlooked, source of inner richness. This internal state acts as a powerful counterpoint to the insatiable desires fueled by consumer culture and the pervasive belief that happiness is inextricably linked to material acquisition. By focusing on gratitude for what is already present, we can dismantle the psychological scaffolding that drives endless consumption.

Consider the psychological impact of cultivating gratitude. When we make a conscious effort to acknowledge the good in our lives, no matter how small, we shift our focus from scarcity to abundance. This simple act can recalibrate our perception of wealth. Instead of viewing our financial situation through the lens of what is missing – the next promotion, the larger house, the fancier car – we begin to see what is present: a roof over our heads, food on the table, meaningful relationships, health, and perhaps even the simple pleasure of a sunny day. This conscious appreciation of existing blessings builds a powerful inner resilience, making us less susceptible to the manufactured desires that marketing and societal pressures constantly thrust upon us.

It is the bedrock upon which a truly rich life, independent of external validation, is built.

The relentless pursuit of "more" is a treadmill that never stops. No matter how much one acquires, there is always a new benchmark to reach, a newer model to desire, a more extravagant lifestyle to emulate. This can create a self-perpetuating cycle of dissatisfaction. The joy derived from a new purchase often proves fleeting, quickly replaced by the anticipation of the next acquisition. This hamster wheel of desire can trap individuals in a state of perpetual wanting, where true fulfillment remains just out of reach, always promised by the next potential purchase, the next financial milestone. Contentment, conversely, offers an escape from this treadmill. It is the realization that happiness is not a destination to be reached through accumulation, but a state of being that can be cultivated in the here and now.

Moreover, contentment fosters a profound sense of peace that is often absent in the lives of those solely focused on external validation. The anxiety associated with maintaining a certain lifestyle, the fear of falling behind, and the pressure to keep up with perceived societal standards can create a significant mental burden. When contentment becomes a guiding principle, these pressures begin to dissipate. One is no longer driven by the need to impress others or to conform to external definitions of success. Instead, the focus shifts inward, towards personal well-being, genuine happiness, and the quiet satisfaction of living a life aligned with one's authentic values. This inner peace is, in itself, a form of wealth that cannot be measured in monetary terms.

The ability to find happiness and satisfaction regardless of one's material possessions is a cornerstone of genuine wealth. Many individuals amass significant fortunes, only to find themselves hollow and unfulfilled. They may have the financial means to purchase anything they desire, yet they lack the inner peace and sense of sufficiency that truly defines a rich life. This is where contentment shines. It teaches us that true wealth is not about what we own, but about how we feel about what we have and who we are. It is the profound understanding that our inner state is far more powerful than any external circumstance.

Consider the concept of opportunity cost, not just in terms of money, but in terms of life. Every hour spent chasing a higher salary, every dollar spent on a status symbol that doesn't truly resonate, is an hour or a dollar that could have been invested in experiences, relationships, personal growth, or simply in moments of quiet reflection. Contentment allows us to make more discerning choices about how we invest our most precious resources – our time and energy.

When we are content, we are less likely to be swayed by the superficial allure of what others have or what advertising suggests we should want. We can more easily identify what truly adds value to our lives and dedicate ourselves to those pursuits.

The antidote to consumerism lies in cultivating an internal locus of control regarding happiness. Consumer culture is designed to externalize happiness, making us believe that it is something to be purchased. Advertisers skillfully tap into our desires for belonging, status, security, and pleasure, positioning their products as the key to unlocking these states. Contentment, however, recognizes that these essential human needs are best met through internal cultivation and meaningful connections. It empowers individuals to see through the manufactured desires and to seek fulfillment from sources that are sustainable and genuinely nourishing.

This internal shift also allows for a more mindful approach to spending, as discussed previously. When contentment is present, the impulse to make unnecessary purchases diminishes. The desire for a new gadget or a trendy item loses its power when one is already satisfied with what they have and what brings them genuine joy. This doesn't mean abstaining from all purchases; rather, it means that spending becomes more intentional, more aligned with true needs and values, rather than being a reaction to external stimuli or an attempt to fill an emotional void. Each purchase is made from a place of sufficiency, not deficiency.

The ability to be grateful for small things is a powerful wealth-building habit, irrespective of financial status. The simple act of savoring a meal, enjoying a conversation with a loved one, or appreciating the beauty of nature can provide immense satisfaction. These are experiences that cost little to nothing but offer immeasurable returns in terms of happiness and well-being. By actively seeking out and appreciating these moments, we train our minds to recognize and value the abundance that already surrounds us. This practice directly counteracts the constant urge for more that characterizes a discontented mindset.

Furthermore, contentment fosters a sense of financial freedom that is distinct from mere financial independence. While financial independence is the state of having sufficient income to live without working, true financial freedom, enriched by contentment, is the absence of financial anxiety and the freedom from being controlled by one's desires. When one is content, the pressure to earn more simply to fund an ever-expanding list of wants is significantly reduced. This allows for greater flexibility in career choices, a willingness to take calculated risks, and the ability to prioritize personal fulfillment over purely financial gain. It liberates individuals from the gilded cage of endless accumulation.

Imagine two individuals with identical financial resources. One is constantly worried about losing it all, always striving for the next level of perceived security, driven by a fear of scarcity. The other, while financially prudent, finds joy in their current circumstances, appreciating the security they have built, and finding satisfaction in experiences and relationships. The latter individual, though possessing the same material wealth, is undeniably richer due to their state of contentment. Their wealth is not solely measured by their net worth, but by their peace of mind and their capacity for joy.

The pursuit of contentment requires a conscious and ongoing effort to shift our focus. It involves actively practicing mindfulness, cultivating gratitude, and critically examining the narratives that surround wealth and happiness. It is a journey of self-discovery, where we learn to distinguish between true needs and manufactured wants, and where we come to understand that our inner state is the ultimate determinant of our well-being. By embracing contentment, we redefine wealth not as the abundance of possessions, but as the abundance of a fulfilling and joyful life, lived with peace and sufficiency.

This internal redefinition of wealth is crucial in navigating the complexities of modern financial life. We are constantly bombarded with messages that equate success with consumerism and that frame dissatisfaction as a necessary precursor to progress. Contentment offers a powerful alternative. It suggests that true progress lies not in acquiring more, but in appreciating what we have, in nurturing our inner lives, and in finding joy in the present moment.

This perspective not only leads to greater personal happiness but also to a more sustainable and ethical approach to finance, one that prioritizes well-being over endless accumulation.

Ultimately, contentment is not about settling or becoming complacent. It is about recognizing that the most valuable aspects of life – love, connection, health, purpose, and inner peace – are not inherently tied to material wealth. By cultivating a deep sense of appreciation for what we have, we build a foundation of resilience that can withstand the inevitable ups and downs of financial life.

We become less susceptible to the pressures of consumerism and more empowered to make choices that align with our true values and aspirations. This inner state of sufficiency is the most profound and enduring form of wealth we can ever achieve, a richness that money simply cannot buy. It allows us to live a life that is not just financially prudent, but genuinely abundant in spirit and purpose, leading to a more peaceful, fulfilling, and truly wealthy existence.

Avoiding the Pitfalls of Overspending

The siren song of consumerism is a powerful force, skillfully orchestrated to play upon our deepest desires and insecurities. We are bombarded daily with messages that equate happiness with acquisition, progress with possession, and belonging with brand affiliation. Understanding the insidious mechanisms behind overspending is the first crucial step in fortifying our financial foundations. These aren't merely passive temptations; they are active, calculated strategies designed to part us from our hard-earned money, often leaving us with regret and financial strain.

One of the most potent psychological triggers for overspending is the **fear of missing out (FOMO)**. This pervasive anxiety, amplified by social media and the constant showcasing of others' perceived experiences and possessions, creates a sense of urgency to acquire. We see curated images of exotic vacations, the latest gadgets, or trendy fashion, and an insidious thought creeps in: if I don't have this, I'm somehow falling behind, or worse, I'm not living my life to its fullest potential. This fear isn't rooted in genuine need, but in a manufactured sense of inadequacy. The solution lies in recognizing that curated online lives are rarely the full reality and that true fulfillment comes from within, not from keeping pace with a digitally amplified illusion. By consciously limiting exposure to triggers that induce FOMO, such as social media scrolling, and focusing on gratitude for our own circumstances, we can begin to dismantle its hold.

Closely related is the concept of **emotional spending**. Many of us reach for our wallets when we're feeling stressed, sad, bored, or even overly excited. A new purchase can provide a temporary dopamine hit, a fleeting sense of comfort or control. This is akin to using a credit card as an emotional crutch. The immediate gratification can mask underlying emotional issues, but it does nothing to address them. In fact, the subsequent financial stress can exacerbate negative emotions. Developing emotional intelligence and healthy coping mechanisms for stress, sadness, or boredom is paramount. This might involve journaling, exercise, meditation, or talking to a trusted friend or therapist. When we feel the urge to shop to cope with an emotion, pausing, identifying the underlying feeling, and choosing a non-spending coping strategy can significantly curb impulsive buying.

Societal pressure and the "keeping up with the Joneses" mentality are also significant drivers of overspending. We live in a culture that often associates financial success with outward displays of wealth. This can manifest in buying a larger house than we need, a more expensive car than is practical, or constantly upgrading electronics to match our neighbors or colleagues. The underlying message is that our worth is somehow tied to our possessions. Breaking free from this requires a conscious decision to define success on our own terms, rather than by external benchmarks. It involves cultivating a strong sense of self-worth that is independent of material possessions and focusing on personal values and goals, rather than perceived social expectations. When we prioritize experiences, personal growth, and meaningful relationships over material status symbols, we naturally reduce the pressure to overspend.

Marketing and advertising are masters at creating perceived needs and amplifying desires. Advertisers are incredibly skilled at tapping into our emotional vulnerabilities, linking their products to concepts like happiness, success, love, and security. They employ sophisticated psychological techniques, from creating a sense of urgency ("limited time offer!") to associating products with aspirational lifestyles. Understanding these tactics is a powerful defense. Recognizing that advertisements are designed to persuade, not inform, and questioning the underlying message – "Do I truly need this, or am I being convinced I do?" – can be incredibly effective. Developing a critical eye towards advertising allows us to see through the persuasive narratives and make purchasing decisions based on genuine needs and values.

The ease of **credit and 'buy now, pay later' schemes** is another significant pitfall. The availability of credit can create an illusion of affordability, decoupling the act of purchase from the immediate pain of parting with cash. When you can acquire something instantly without feeling the direct impact on your bank account, it becomes much easier to overspend. 'Buy now, pay later' services, while offering convenience, can mask the true cost of purchases and make it harder to track overall spending. It's crucial to remember that credit is not free money. It is borrowed money that needs to be repaid, often with interest.

Practicing a "cash-only" approach for non-essential purchases or at least limiting the use of credit cards to what you can afford to pay off in full each month, can be a powerful way to stay grounded and avoid accumulating debt.

The **lack of a clear budget and financial goals** leaves individuals adrift in a sea of potential spending opportunities without a compass. Without knowing where your money is going and what you are saving for, it's easy to spend impulsively on things that don't align with your long-term objectives. A well-defined budget acts as a roadmap, guiding your spending and ensuring that your financial resources are allocated purposefully. Setting clear, achievable financial goals – whether it's saving for a down payment, building an emergency fund, or investing for retirement – provides motivation and a framework for making wise spending decisions. When faced with an impulse purchase, asking yourself if it aligns with your goals can be a powerful deterrent.

The allure of **convenience and instant gratification** often leads to overspending. Paying a premium for pre-cut vegetables, pre-packaged meals, or express shipping might seem like a small price to pay for time saved, but these small expenses can add up significantly over time. While convenience has its place, consistently opting for the more expensive, convenient option over more budget-friendly alternatives can erode your financial health. Practicing delayed gratification, which involves resisting the urge for immediate rewards in favor of longer-term benefits, is a crucial skill. This might mean grabbing a cookbook like "*Viewing Food Through the Lens of Nourishment*" and cooking nutritious meals at home instead of eating out, shopping for groceries with a list and sticking to it or waiting for sales on items you need.

Another common pitfall is the **"sunk cost fallacy"** in spending. This refers to the tendency to continue investing time or money into something simply because you've already invested in it, even if it's no longer a rational decision. For example, continuing to use a membership or subscription you no longer use because you've already paid for it, or buying accessories for a gadget you rarely use. It's important to evaluate purchases and commitments based on their current and future value, not on past investments. If something is no longer serving you or aligning with your needs, it's often more prudent to cut your losses, even if it means accepting that the initial investment was not as beneficial as hoped.

We also fall prey to **"novelty seeking"** – the inherent human desire for new experiences and things. While this can drive innovation and personal growth, it can also lead to unnecessary spending on the latest trends, gadgets, or upgrades. The excitement of something new is often short-lived, quickly replaced by the desire for the *next* new thing. To combat this, cultivate appreciation for what you already have. Engage in mindful consumption, questioning whether a new purchase will truly enhance your life or simply satisfy a fleeting desire for novelty. Sometimes, rediscovering or repurposing your already existing items can be just as satisfying and far more financially responsible than you think.

The act of **comparison** fuels much of our unnecessary spending. Constantly comparing our lives, our possessions, and our achievements to others, often through the lens of social media, is a recipe for discontent and overspending. This comparison trap can lead to feelings of inadequacy and a drive to acquire things to 'keep up.' The antidote is to focus inward, to cultivate self-awareness, and to appreciate your unique journey. Practicing gratitude for what you have, rather than envying what others possess, shifts your mindset from scarcity to abundance. When you are secure in your own path, the desire to measure your success against others diminishes significantly.

Furthermore, a lack of **financial literacy** can inadvertently lead to overspending. Not fully understanding concepts like interest rates, inflation, or the true cost of borrowing can result in decisions that are detrimental to long-term financial health. Taking the time to educate yourself about personal finance, budgeting, saving, and investing is an investment in itself. Resources such as books like "*Unlocking Your All*", reputable financial websites, workshops, and even qualified financial advisors can provide the knowledge needed to make informed decisions and avoid common spending pitfalls.

To actively avoid these pitfalls, several strategies can be employed. Firstly, **implement a "cooling-off period"** for non-essential purchases. Before buying something that isn't a necessity, give yourself *24* hours, or even a week, to think about it. During this time, ask yourself if you genuinely need the item, if you can afford it without compromising your budget, and if it aligns with your long-term financial goals. Often, the urge to buy will pass.

Secondly, **unfollow or mute social media accounts** that consistently trigger FOMO or promote excessive consumerism. Curate your digital environment to support your financial goals, not undermine them. Surround yourself with content that inspires and educates, rather than feeds discontent.

Thirdly, **practice conscious consumption**. Before buying anything, ask yourself: "Do I truly need this? Will this add lasting value to my life? Can I find a more affordable or sustainable alternative?" This mindful approach shifts spending from an automatic reaction to a deliberate choice.

Fourthly, **create and stick to a realistic budget**. This involves tracking your income and expenses, allocating funds for different categories (housing, food, transportation, savings, entertainment), and regularly reviewing your spending to ensure you are staying on track. Tools like budgeting apps or simple spreadsheets can be invaluable.

Fifthly, **automate your savings**. Treat saving as a non-negotiable expense. Set up automatic transfers from your checking account to your savings or investment accounts each payday. This "pay yourself first" strategy ensures that you are consistently building your financial future before you have the opportunity to spend the money.

Sixthly, **learn to distinguish between needs and wants**. While wants are desires that enhance life, needs are essential for survival and well-being. Prioritizing needs over wants, especially during the initial stages of building financial prudence, is crucial.

Seventhly, **seek value, not just low prices**. While saving money is important, sometimes paying a bit more for a higher-quality item that lasts longer can be more cost-effective in the long run than repeatedly buying cheaper, inferior products.

Eighthly, **find joy in experiences rather than possessions**. Invest your time and money in activities, learning, and relationships that bring genuine, lasting happiness, rather than temporary satisfaction from material goods. Travel, hobbies, education, and spending time with loved ones are often far more rewarding.

Finally, and perhaps most importantly, **cultivate self-compassion**. You will likely make spending mistakes along the way. Instead of dwelling on guilt, learn from these experiences, adjust your strategies, and move forward with renewed commitment. Financial prudence is a journey, not a destination, and a forgiving mindset is essential for sustained progress. By understanding the psychological, social, and marketing forces that drive overspending, and by implementing practical strategies to counteract them, you can build a robust financial foundation, protect your peace of mind, and achieve true financial well-being. This conscious effort to control your spending is a fundamental pillar of financial prudence, setting the stage for greater security and freedom.

Financial Prudence as a Virtue

Financial prudence, at its core, transcends the mere act of budgeting or saving; it is an ethical compass guiding our financial decisions and shaping our character. When we adopt a stance of living within our means, we are not simply making a pragmatic choice for personal gain but engaging in a principled behavior that reflects deeper virtues. This deliberate approach to managing resources speaks volumes about our integrity, our capacity for discipline, and our commitment to foresight. It is a conscious decision to align our actions with our values, recognizing that our financial stewardship has implications that extend beyond our personal balance sheets, touching upon our relationships, our communities, and even our very sense of self.

Consider integrity. True integrity in financial matters means being honest with ourselves about our income, our expenses, and our capacities. It means not deluding ourselves into believing we can afford something we cannot or making commitments that we know we are unlikely to keep. When we consistently spend less than we earn, we are demonstrating a fundamental honesty with ourselves and, by extension, with others who might rely on us or be affected by our financial decisions. This is not about deprivation; it is about authenticity. It is about acknowledging reality and acting in accordance with it, rather than chasing fleeting desires that lead to debt and compromise. This commitment to truthfulness in our financial dealings builds a bedrock of self-respect and fosters trust in our relationships. It means saying "no" to impulse buys that strain our resources, not out of weakness, but out of a strength of character that prioritizes long-term stability and adherence to our commitments. This consistent practice of honest self-assessment and responsible action cultivates a reputation for reliability, which is invaluable in both personal and professional spheres. It is the quiet but powerful message that we are dependable, that our word carries weight, and that our financial behavior is a reflection of our reliable character of us all.

Discipline is another virtue deeply intertwined with financial prudence. The ability to defer gratification, to resist immediate temptations in favor of future security and well-being, is a hallmark of a disciplined mind. This self-control is not innate for most; it is a muscle that must be developed and strengthened through practice. Every time we choose to save a portion of our income instead of spending it, every time we resist an impulse purchase because it deviates from our budget or our goals, we are exercising this crucial virtue. This discipline extends to every aspect of our financial lives, from meticulously tracking our expenses to consistently contributing to savings and investment accounts. It means waking up to the reality of our financial situation day after day, making conscious choices that support our long-term objectives, even when easier, more gratifying alternatives present themselves. This consistent application of willpower builds resilience, enabling us to navigate economic fluctuations and unexpected challenges with greater confidence. It teaches us that true freedom often comes not from unrestrained spending, but from the freedom that comes with knowing our finances are under control, allowing us to make choices based on desire, not necessity. The act of consistently making responsible financial choices, even when difficult, reinforces our sense of agency and capability, fostering a deep inner strength that permeates other areas of life.

Foresight, the ability to anticipate future needs and consequences, is also a cornerstone of financial prudence. It involves looking beyond the present moment and considering how our current financial decisions will impact our future selves. This means building an emergency fund to prepare for unforeseen job loss or medical emergencies, saving for retirement to ensure financial security in our later years, and investing wisely to grow our wealth over time. It's about understanding that the present comfort derived from excessive spending can lead to future hardship, and conversely, that present sacrifice can yield future abundance and peace of mind. This forward-thinking approach allows us to not only avoid potential pitfalls but also to proactively create opportunities for ourselves and our families. It is the antithesis of a reactive, spend-as-you-go mentality. Instead, it is a proactive stance that acknowledges that life is unpredictable and that preparing for the future is not just wise, but a moral imperative for self-reliance and for the well-being of those dependent on us. This foresight also enables us to approach life's milestones – education, homeownership, travel, or supporting loved ones – with a sense of preparedness and confidence, rather than anxiety and uncertainty.

Living within our means, therefore, is not merely a financial strategy; it is a principled commitment to a life of integrity, discipline, and foresight. It is a declaration that we value stability over superficiality, long-term security over fleeting gratification, and responsible self-reliance over burdensome dependency. This commitment fosters personal stability, creating a sense of control and peace of mind that is often elusive in the lives of those who struggle with financial mismanagement. When our expenses are aligned with our income, we are less susceptible to stress, anxiety, and the emotional turmoil that debt can bring. This internal stability then radiates outward, strengthening our relationships and our ability to contribute positively to our communities.

Furthermore, by living within our means, we actively reduce our reliance on others. This independence is not born of isolation, but of a healthy self-sufficiency. It means being able to meet our own needs and support ourselves without becoming a burden on family, friends, or social welfare systems. This capacity for self-reliance is a powerful affirmation of personal agency and contributes to a more resilient society. When individuals are financially stable, they are better equipped to handle personal crises without overwhelming their support networks. They can also participate more fully in their communities, whether through charitable giving, volunteerism, or simply by being a stable presence. This conscious choice to manage our finances responsibly is a direct contribution to collective well-being. It fosters a culture of responsibility and mutual respect, where individuals are empowered to manage their own lives and contribute positively to the fabric of society. It shifts the focus from entitlement or expectation to contribution and self-governance, strengthening the bonds of community through shared principles of integrity and accountability.

Viewing our financial habits as a reflection of our values transforms the often-mundane task of managing money into a profound exercise in self-discovery and ethical living. It asks us to consider what truly matters: Is it the latest gadget, the designer label, or the fleeting thrill of acquisition? Or is it the security of a stable home, the freedom to pursue our passions without financial constraint, the ability to support our loved ones, and the peace of mind that comes from knowing we are living honorably and responsibly? When we align our spending with our deepest values, our financial decisions become a powerful statement about who we are and what we stand for. This alignment cultivates a sense of purpose and fulfillment that material possessions alone can never provide. It allows us to build a life that is not just financially sound, but also meaningful and ethically grounded. By embracing financial prudence as a virtue, we not only secure our own futures but also contribute to a more stable, responsible, and resilient world, demonstrating that true wealth lies not just in what we accumulate, but in how we live and how we impact others. This ethical dimension of financial prudence underscores the profound interconnectedness between personal well-being and societal health, elevating the practice from a personal chore to a civic responsibility.

Chapter 3: Cultivating Personal Happiness and Well-being

The Inner Source of Joy

The journey towards cultivating personal happiness and well-being is, at its heart, an exploration of an inner landscape. While the previous discussions have illuminated the profound impact of financial prudence on our lives, a foundational truth remains: true, enduring joy does not reside in the accumulation of wealth or the favorable configuration of external circumstances. Instead, it is an intrinsic quality, a wellspring that flows from within, accessible to each of us regardless of our material possessions or the vicissitudes of life. This inner source of joy is not a fleeting emotion, but a stable, resilient state of being, cultivated through conscious effort and the adoption of specific internal practices. What I want you to know now it is the recognition that while external factors may influence our mood or immediate comfort, they do not, and cannot, dictate the depth of our contentment.

To understand this inner source, we must first acknowledge a fundamental misconception: that happiness is a destination, a state to be achieved once certain external conditions are met. This pervasive belief often leads us on a relentless pursuit of more – more money, more possessions, more accolades, more experiences – only to find that the promised land of happiness remains perpetually on the horizon. The truth is far more empowering. Happiness, in its most profound and sustainable form, is a practice, a way of being that we can nurture and develop from the inside out. It is about shifting our focus from what we *have* or *lack* in the external world to what we cultivate within our own minds and hearts.

One of the most potent pathways to unlocking this inner source of joy is through the practice of mindfulness. Mindfulness, in essence, is the art of paying attention, on purpose, in the present moment, non-judgmentally. It is about fully engaging with our experiences, noticing our thoughts, feelings, bodily sensations, and the surrounding environment without labeling them as good or bad, right or wrong. When we are mindful, we are not lost in rumination about the past or anxious anticipation of the future. Instead, we are grounded in the here and now, fully alive to the richness of each moment. This practice can be as simple as savoring the taste of a meal, truly listening to a conversation, or feeling the warmth of the sun on your skin. Each instance of mindful presence anchors us to reality, quieting the internal chatter that often fuels dissatisfaction and discontent. By consistently bringing our awareness back to the present, we begin to decouple our emotional state from external triggers, realizing that we have the capacity to choose how we respond to our experiences, rather than being passively swept away by them. This conscious choice to inhabit the present moment is a powerful act of reclaiming our inner peace, fostering a sense of calm and clarity that is the bedrock of sustained happiness. The benefits of mindfulness extend beyond immediate calm; research in neuroscience has shown that regular mindfulness practice can lead to structural changes in the brain, strengthening areas associated with emotional regulation, attention, and self-awareness. This neural rewiring further empowers our ability to access and cultivate inner joy, creating a positive feedback loop where mindful moments lead to greater capacity for mindful living.

Complementing mindfulness is the practice of self-compassion. In a world that often encourages self-criticism and the relentless pursuit of perfection, self-compassion offers a gentle antidote. It involves treating ourselves with the same kindness, understanding, and acceptance that we would offer to a dear friend who is struggling. This means acknowledging our imperfections, our mistakes, and our moments of difficulty without harsh judgment. It is recognizing that suffering and failure are part of the human experience, and that in these moments, we are not alone but connected to the shared human condition. Self-compassion is not about making excuses for our behavior or lowering our standards. Rather, it is about creating a supportive inner environment that allows for growth and healing. When we are self-compassionate, we are less likely to be paralyzed by fear of failure, more willing to take risks, and more resilient in the face of setbacks. This internal kindness fosters a sense of safety and acceptance, creating the fertile ground from which genuine joy can blossom. Imagine a gardener who meticulously tends to their plants, providing water, sunlight, and nutrients. Self-compassion is the internal equivalent, nurturing our inner self, allowing our innate capacity for happiness to flourish. It's about understanding that the journey of personal growth is rarely linear, and that moments of stumbles are opportunities for learning and self-discovery, not reasons for self-condemnation.

Gratitude serves as another vital pillar in building our inner reservoir of joy. It is the conscious appreciation for the good things in our lives, both big and small. This can range from profound thankfulness for loved ones and good health to simple appreciation for a beautiful sunset or a warm cup of tea. The act of intentionally recognizing and acknowledging these blessings shifts our focus away from what we perceive as lacking and towards what we already possess. Gratitude is a powerful redirector of our attention, training our minds to seek out the positive aspects of our reality. Regularly practicing gratitude, perhaps through journaling or a daily mental inventory, can profoundly impact our emotional state. It interrupts negative thought patterns, reduces feelings of envy and resentment, and cultivates a sense of abundance. When we are genuinely grateful, we are less driven by the need for external validation or material acquisition, as our sense of fulfillment is rooted in an appreciation for what is already present. This practice is not about ignoring challenges or difficulties, but about maintaining perspective and recognizing that even amidst adversity, there are elements for which to be thankful. It's about acknowledging the inherent goodness that exists, even when it's not immediately obvious.

The interconnectedness of these practices – mindfulness, self-compassion, and gratitude – creates a virtuous cycle that strengthens our inner capacity for happiness. As we become more mindful, we notice more opportunities for gratitude and approach ourselves with greater kindness. As we practice self-compassion, we become more open to accepting our present circumstances, which in turn allows for more mindful awareness and genuine gratitude. And as we cultivate gratitude, we often find ourselves more present and more accepting of ourselves and our experiences.

This synergy means that progress in one area naturally supports growth in the others, creating a robust internal framework for well-being.

Psychological research consistently supports the notion that internal states are more influential in determining happiness than external conditions. Studies on hedonic adaptation, for instance, reveal that we tend to return to a relatively stable level of happiness despite major positive or negative events or life changes. This means that while a new car or a promotion might bring a temporary boost in happiness, the effect often fades as we adapt to the new reality. This adaptation process highlights the ephemeral nature of happiness derived solely from external sources. Conversely, practices that foster internal resilience and contentment, such as mindfulness and gratitude, tend to have a more lasting impact. They build an internal capacity to weather life's storms and to appreciate the everyday moments, leading to a more stable and profound sense of well-being.

This understanding empowers us to invest our energy not in the endless pursuit of external markers of success, but in the cultivation of our inner world, which offers a far more reliable and fulfilling path to happiness.

Consider the story of a person who, despite achieving significant financial success and material comfort, remains perpetually unhappy, always searching for the "next big thing" to bring them fulfillment. Their focus is on acquisition, on what is *not yet* theirs, leading to a constant state of longing. In contrast, imagine someone with modest means who finds profound joy in their relationships, their creative pursuits, and their ability to contribute to their community. Their happiness is not contingent on their bank balance; it is derived from a rich inner life and a deep appreciation for the present moment. This contrast illustrates the power of cultivating an inner source of joy, demonstrating that our perception and our internal state are far more influential than our external circumstances. The external world can provide fleeting pleasures, but it is the cultivation of inner contentment that offers lasting joy and resilience.

Furthermore, the ability to find joy within is deeply intertwined with our sense of autonomy and self-efficacy. When we understand that our happiness is not dependent on external forces or the approval of others, we reclaim our power. We are no longer beholden to the whims of fortune or the opinions of society. This sense of inner control and agency is incredibly empowering and is a significant contributor to overall well-being. It allows us to make choices that align with our values and our authentic selves, rather than simply reacting to external pressures. This internal locus of control is a cornerstone of psychological resilience, enabling us to navigate challenges with confidence and to savor moments of success with genuine appreciation. It fosters a sense of purpose and meaning, as we are actively shaping our own experience of life.

The development of an inner source of joy also requires a willingness to engage with our own inner world, including our less comfortable emotions. Suppressing or avoiding difficult feelings like sadness, anger, or fear often leads to them festering and growing, ultimately hindering our capacity for joy. Instead, a mature approach involves acknowledging these emotions, understanding their origins, and allowing them to pass without judgment. Mindfulness, again, plays a crucial role here, enabling us to observe these emotions without becoming overwhelmed by them. Self-compassion is essential for navigating these internal experiences with kindness rather than self-criticism. When we learn to hold our difficult emotions with acceptance, we create space for more positive experiences to co-exist, rather than believing that we must be happy *all the time*. This balanced perspective is far more realistic and ultimately, more conducive to lasting well-being. It's about building emotional intelligence, the capacity to understand and manage our own emotions, and to recognize and influence the emotions of others. This is a lifelong skill that deepens our connection to ourselves and to the world around us, providing a stable foundation for happiness.

In essence, the cultivation of personal happiness and well-being is an inward journey.

While external factors play a role in our lives, the most profound and sustainable joy originates from within. By consciously practicing mindfulness, self-compassion, and gratitude, we build a resilient inner landscape that can withstand the inevitable challenges of life. This internal cultivation empowers us to live more fully in the present, to appreciate what we have, and to approach ourselves and our experiences with kindness and acceptance. It is a shift from a consumerist approach to happiness, where we seek it externally, to a generative approach, where we create it from within. This inner source of joy is not a finite resource; it is one that grows and deepens with consistent practice, offering a pathway to a richer, more fulfilling, and truly happier life, irrespective of the circumstances that surround us. It is the realization that the most valuable treasures are not found in external vaults, but within the infinite capacity of the human spirit.

The Gratitude Practice for a Richer Life

The deliberate cultivation of gratitude serves as a potent catalyst for a richer, more vibrant life. Beyond mere politeness or social convention, gratitude is a profound internal practice that reorients our perspective, allowing us to perceive the abundance that already exists, often obscured by our focus on what we lack. It is an active choice to acknowledge and appreciate the positive aspects of our existence, however small they may seem.

This conscious appreciation acts as an anchor, grounding us in the present and pulling us away from the gravitational pull of dissatisfaction and longing that so often characterizes a life lived in pursuit of an elusive future happiness. By consistently engaging in gratitude practices, we effectively retrain our minds to seek out and savor the good, creating a powerful feedback loop that amplifies positive emotions and fosters a deeper sense of contentment.

One of the most accessible and impactful ways to integrate gratitude into your daily life is through the practice of gratitude journaling. This involves setting aside a few moments each day, perhaps in the morning or before bed, to write down a specific number of things for which you are thankful. This number can be as simple as three, or it can be more, depending on your preference and the time you have available. The key is consistency and specificity. Instead of a vague entry like "I'm grateful for my family," a more powerful entry might read, "I'm grateful for the way my partner made me laugh this morning by telling me a silly story about their day, reminding me of our shared sense of humor." This level of detail engages your memory and emotions more deeply, making the experience of gratitude more potent. Over time, this practice not only helps you identify the positive elements in your life but also begins to shift your default mode of thinking. You start to proactively look for things to be grateful for, anticipating the act of writing them down. This simple habit can fundamentally alter your outlook, moving you from a scarcity mindset to an abundance mindset, where you recognize the plentiful gifts that surround you. Consider the cumulative effect: if you commit to listing just three specific things each day, over a year, you will have acknowledged *1,095* distinct instances of good fortune or simple pleasures. This consistent accumulation of positive focus can have a profound impact on your overall well-being and resilience.

Beyond the written word, mindful appreciation offers another powerful avenue for cultivating gratitude. This involves bringing your full, non-judgmental attention to the present moment and the experiences within it. It's about savoring the sensory details, the emotional nuances, and the overall feeling associated with a particular moment or object of appreciation. For instance, when enjoying a cup of coffee, instead of rushing through it while distracted by your to-do list, take a moment to truly experience it. Notice the warmth of the mug in your hands, the rich aroma, the nuanced flavors as you sip, and the comforting sensation as it warms you from the inside out. This practice elevates ordinary experiences into moments of profound gratitude. It's about recognizing that even the most mundane aspects of our lives can be sources of joy and thankfulness if we only choose to pay attention. This mindful engagement extends to all aspects of life: the feeling of clean sheets on your bed, the efficiency of a well-functioning appliance, the simple act of breathing in fresh air, or the comfort of a supportive chair. Each of these can become a focal point for gratitude, transforming your perception of your daily environment and enriching your inner landscape. The beauty of mindful appreciation lies in its adaptability; it can be woven into almost any activity, turning routine into ritual and transforming the mundane into the magnificent.

Expressing gratitude directly to others is equally crucial and often yields a powerful reciprocal effect, strengthening relationships and fostering a more positive social environment. This can take many forms, from a heartfelt "thank you" after someone has helped you, to a more formal letter or email expressing appreciation for their contributions, to a thoughtful gift or gesture of kindness. The act of vocalizing or demonstrating your appreciation not only acknowledges the effort or kindness of the recipient but also reinforces your own feelings of gratitude. It's a way of sharing the positive energy and creating a ripple effect of goodwill. Think about a time someone genuinely thanked you for something you did; how did that make you feel? Often, it feels validating and motivating, encouraging you to continue your positive actions. By extending this courtesy to others, you actively contribute to a more appreciative and connected world, while simultaneously deepening your own sense of thankfulness for the people in your life.

It's about recognizing the value and impact others have on our lives and taking the time to acknowledge it, rather than assuming they already know. This outward expression of gratitude can transform interactions, build stronger bonds, and create a more supportive community.

The impact of consistently practicing gratitude on mental and emotional health is significant and well-documented. Research consistently shows that individuals who regularly practice gratitude tend to experience higher levels of positive emotions, optimism, and overall life satisfaction. They are also found to be more resilient in the face of adversity, better able to cope with stress, and less prone to feelings of envy, resentment, and regret. This is because gratitude actively counters the human tendency towards negativity bias, our innate inclination to focus on threats and problems. By consciously shifting our attention to what is good, we weaken the hold of negative thought patterns and create a more balanced and positive internal dialogue. For instance, someone facing a job loss might, through gratitude journaling, still acknowledge the difficulty of the situation but also find thankfulness for the severance package, the support of friends and family, and the opportunity to re-evaluate their career path. This balanced perspective does not negate the challenges but rather provides the emotional and mental fortitude to navigate them more effectively. It's about finding the silver lining, not as a form of denial, but as a conscious act of self-preservation and emotional well-being.

Consider the real-life example of Sarah, a single mother working two jobs to make ends meet. By all external measures, her life was filled with challenges and financial strain. However, Sarah made a conscious effort to practice gratitude daily. She would write in her journal each night, not about the bills she had to pay, but about the small victories: her son's proud smile when he brought home a good report card, the unexpected kindness of a stranger who paid for her coffee, the quiet moments of peace she found reading a book after her children were asleep. She also made it a point to express her gratitude to her employer for the opportunity to work, to her neighbors for watching her children occasionally, and to her own mother for her unwavering support. Over time, Sarah noticed a profound shift in her outlook. While her external circumstances hadn't magically changed, her internal experience of them had transformed. She felt less overwhelmed and more empowered, capable of facing her daily challenges with a sense of hope and resilience. Her gratitude practice didn't erase her problems, but it gave her the inner strength to manage them, transforming her perception of her life from one of burden to one of blessing. This illustrates how gratitude can be a powerful tool for emotional regulation, enabling individuals to find joy and meaning even amidst difficult circumstances.

The principle of gratitude extends beyond personal well-being to positively influence our relationships and interactions with the wider world. When we cultivate a grateful mindset, we are more likely to approach others with kindness, empathy, and understanding. We become more attuned to the contributions of others, both big and small, and more willing to reciprocate their generosity. This can lead to stronger, more fulfilling relationships, built on a foundation of mutual appreciation and respect. For example, in a professional setting, a manager who regularly expresses gratitude for their team's hard work and dedication often fosters a more positive and productive work environment. Employees who feel seen and valued are more likely to be engaged, motivated, and loyal. Similarly, in personal relationships, expressing appreciation for a partner's efforts, a friend's listening ear, or a family member's support can significantly strengthen those bonds. It creates a positive feedback loop where appreciation breeds more appreciation, leading to deeper connections and a more harmonious existence. This outward projection of gratitude cultivates a more positive and supportive social fabric, benefiting not only the individual but also those around them.

Furthermore, the practice of gratitude can serve as a powerful antidote to materialism and the relentless pursuit of "more." In a society that often equates happiness with possessions and achievements, gratitude reminds us that true fulfillment comes from appreciating what we already have, rather than constantly striving for what we don't. This shift in focus can liberate us from the endless cycle of desire and consumption, allowing us to find contentment in simplicity and in the richness of our experiences and relationships. When we are genuinely grateful for the roof over our heads, the food on our table, and the people in our lives, the allure of material possessions diminishes. We begin to understand that happiness is not contingent on owning the latest gadget or achieving the next milestone, but on cultivating an inner state of appreciation and contentment. This perspective fosters a more sustainable and ethical approach to consumption, encouraging us to value quality over quantity and to recognize the interconnectedness of our choices with the well-being of others and the planet. Gratitude, in this sense, is not just a personal practice but a pathway to a more conscious and fulfilling way of living.

Incorporating gratitude into your life doesn't require grand gestures or significant time commitments. It can be as simple as taking a moment before each meal to silently acknowledge the nourishment it provides or sending a quick text message to a friend to thank them for a recent conversation. The key is consistency and intention. Make it a conscious, deliberate practice.

Start small, perhaps with a daily gratitude journal, and gradually expand your practice to include mindful appreciation of everyday moments and the expression of thanks to others. Remember that gratitude is not about ignoring difficulties or pretending everything is perfect. It is about acknowledging the good that exists alongside the challenges, finding the light even when shadows are present. By making gratitude a regular part of your life, you are not just improving your mood; you are actively building a more resilient, joyful, and deeply satisfying existence. It is an investment in your own well-being, a powerful tool for unlocking a richer, more fulfilling life, built not on what you can acquire, but on what you can truly appreciate. The cumulative effect of these small, consistent acts of thankfulness can lead to a profound transformation, enabling you to navigate life's complexities with grace, find joy in the ordinary, and build a life that is truly rich in meaning and contentment.

Mindful Living Presence in Every Moment

The preceding exploration has illuminated the transformative power of gratitude, a practice that actively recalibrates our internal landscape to recognize and savor the abundance already present in our lives. We've seen how cultivating thankfulness, whether through journaling, mindful appreciation, or direct expression, can foster resilience, enhance emotional well-being, and deepen our connections with others. However, the cultivation of personal happiness and well-being is a multifaceted endeavor, and just as gratitude anchors us in appreciation, another vital practice allows us to truly inhabit the moments that shape our lives: mindful living, the art of being present.

Mindful living is not about escaping reality or achieving a state of perpetual bliss. Instead, it is about engaging with life as it unfolds, moment by moment, with an open, accepting, and curious awareness. It is the deliberate choice to shift our focus from the distractions of the past and the anxieties of the future to the richness of the *now*. In our fast-paced, hyper-connected world, where notifications ping incessantly and our minds are often a whirlwind of thoughts and to-do lists, the ability to be truly present is becoming an increasingly rare and precious commodity. Yet, it is precisely in these present moments that our lives are actually lived. By learning to inhabit them fully, we can unlock a profound sense of peace, clarity, and contentment.

One of the primary benefits of mindful living is its potent ability to reduce stress. When we are caught in a cycle of worrying about what might happen or regretting what has already occurred, our bodies are often in a state of heightened alert, activating the stress response. Mindfulness offers a powerful antidote to this by gently guiding our attention back to the present. Consider, for instance, the simple act of taking a deep breath. While it sounds elementary, consciously focusing on the sensation of air entering your lungs, filling your chest, and then slowly exhaling can create an immediate physiological shift. This practice, often referred to as mindful breathing, acts as an anchor, pulling you out of the turbulent waters of anxious thoughts and grounding you in the tangible reality of your breath. As you practice this more regularly, you begin to train your mind to recognize when it has wandered into worry and to gently, without judgment, bring it back to the present moment, thereby interrupting the stress cycle before it escalates. This is not about suppressing thoughts, but rather about observing them without getting carried away by them, recognizing them as transient mental events.

Furthermore, mindful living significantly enhances our capacity for emotional regulation. Our emotions, while a vital part of the human experience, can sometimes feel overwhelming. When we react impulsively to strong feelings – be it anger, sadness, or frustration – we often regret our actions later. Mindfulness provides a crucial pause between a stimulus and our response. By bringing awareness to our emotional state without immediate judgment or reaction, we create space to understand what we are feeling and why. This understanding allows us to choose a more constructive and compassionate response. Imagine you receive a critical email at work. Your initial reaction might be anger or defensiveness. However, by practicing mindfulness, you can acknowledge the surge of anger, notice the physical sensations associated with it – perhaps a tightening in your chest or a flushed face – and then choose how to respond rather than being driven by the immediate emotional impulse. This mindful pause allows you to process the information more calmly, consider the sender's perspective, and craft a measured and professional reply, thus preventing an unnecessary conflict and preserving your own sense of composure. This ability to observe emotions without being consumed by them is a cornerstone of emotional intelligence and contributes immensely to our overall well-being.

The practice of mindfulness also serves to deepen our appreciation for everyday experiences. So much of our daily life is filled with routine activities that we perform on autopilot, barely registering their presence. From the morning commute to washing dishes, these moments often pass us by unnoticed. Mindfulness invites us to bring our full attention to these ordinary occurrences, transforming them into opportunities for richer experience. Consider the simple act of eating. When we eat mindlessly, perhaps while scrolling through our phones or watching television, we miss out on the sensory pleasure of the meal. By contrast, a mindful approach to eating involves paying attention to the colors, textures, aromas, and flavors of the food. Notice the warmth of the bowl, the crunch of a vegetable, the satisfying taste of each bite. This heightened sensory awareness not only enhances the enjoyment of the meal but also fosters a sense of gratitude for the nourishment and sustenance it provides, connecting back to the principles of gratitude we've previously discussed. This practice can be applied to virtually any activity, from walking in nature, feeling the ground beneath your feet and the breeze on your skin, to listening to music, truly hearing the nuances of the melody and lyrics. By infusing these mundane moments with conscious attention, we expand our capacity for joy and contentment, realizing that happiness can be found not just in grand events, but in the fabric of our everyday lives.

Integrating mindfulness into our daily routines doesn't require significant time commitments or drastic lifestyle changes. There are numerous accessible techniques that can be woven into the existing structure of our days. One of the most fundamental is mindful breathing, which can be practiced anywhere, anytime. You can dedicate just a few minutes upon waking, before a meal, or during a brief pause in your workday to simply focus on your breath. Another powerful practice is mindful walking.

Instead of rushing from one place to another, try to pay attention to the sensation of your feet making contact with the ground, the rhythm of your steps, and the sights and sounds around you. Even a short walk can become a meditative experience if approached with conscious awareness.

Formal meditation practices, such as sitting meditation, offer a more structured approach to cultivating mindfulness. This involves finding a quiet space, sitting comfortably, and gently focusing your attention on a chosen object, such as the breath, bodily sensations, or a mantra. When your mind inevitably wanders, the practice is not to get frustrated, but to gently acknowledge the thought and then guide your attention back to your chosen anchor. This consistent practice of redirecting your attention strengthens your ability to be present and focused in all areas of your life. Many guided meditation apps and online resources are available to support individuals in establishing a regular meditation practice.

Beyond these formal techniques, mindfulness can also be cultivated through informal practices that are integrated into everyday activities. This might involve simply paying more attention to sensory details throughout your day. For example, when you're brushing your teeth, notice the taste of the toothpaste, the sensation of the bristles, the feeling of the water. When you're in the shower, feel the warmth of the water on your skin, the scent of the soap. These micro-moments of mindful engagement, when practiced consistently, train your brain to be more present and observant, gradually transforming your default mode of operating.

The cumulative effect of these practices is a profound shift in how we experience life. We become less reactive and more responsive, less overwhelmed and more centered. This enhanced presence allows us to connect more deeply with ourselves, our loved ones, and the world around us. It fosters a sense of inner peace that is not dependent on external circumstances, but rather on our internal state of being. By embracing mindful living, we embark on a journey of self-discovery and cultivate a deeper, more sustainable form of happiness and well-being, finding richness and meaning in every moment.

Consider the experience of someone learning to drive. In the initial stages, every action requires intense concentration: checking mirrors, signaling, shifting gears, monitoring speed. The mind is fully engaged with the task at hand, acutely aware of the present moment because the consequences of inattention are significant. Over time, with practice, driving becomes more automatic. The skills are ingrained, and the mind can wander to other thoughts. While this automation is efficient, it can also lead to a disconnection from the experience itself. Mindful driving would involve consciously bringing attention back to the act of driving, even when it feels familiar. Noticing the feel of the steering wheel, the subtle adjustments to maintain lane position, the changing scenery outside the window. This doesn't mean becoming overly anxious or distracted but rather maintaining a state of engaged presence. It's about appreciating the ability to navigate the road, the freedom of movement, and the environment through which you are traveling. This mindful approach to even the most routine activities can elevate them from mundane tasks to opportunities for connection and appreciation.

Another powerful application of mindful living is in how we approach communication and relationships. When we are truly present during conversations, we listen more attentively, we respond more thoughtfully, and we connect more genuinely. Instead of formulating our reply while the other person is still speaking, or being distracted by our own internal monologue, mindful communication involves giving our full attention to the speaker. This means making eye contact, nodding to show engagement, and truly absorbing their words and the emotions behind them. Such presence fosters trust, strengthens bonds, and leads to more meaningful interactions. Think about a time someone genuinely listened to you, without interruption or distraction. How did that make you feel valued and understood? This is the power of mindful presence in relationships. It's about creating a space where others feel heard and seen, and in doing so, you'll be enriching our own experience of connection.

The journey of mindful living is a continuous practice, not a destination. There will be days when our minds feel particularly restless, and moments when distractions seem insurmountable.

The key is not to strive for perfection, but to approach each moment with gentle persistence and self-compassion. When we notice our minds have wandered, we simply acknowledge it and bring our attention back, again and again, with kindness. Each time we do this, we are strengthening the muscle of presence. This iterative process of noticing, acknowledging, and returning is, in itself, a profound practice that cultivates resilience and a deeper understanding of our own minds.

Furthermore, mindful living cultivates a greater capacity for self-compassion. When we are more aware of our thoughts and emotions without judgment, we can begin to extend the same kindness and understanding to ourselves that we might offer to a dear friend. This is particularly important when we make mistakes or experience difficult emotions. Instead of harsh self-criticism, mindfulness encourages us to acknowledge our struggles with a sense of gentle acceptance, recognizing that imperfection is an inherent part of the human condition. This self-compassion is not a sign of weakness, but a source of inner strength, enabling us to navigate challenges with greater resilience and to foster a more positive and supportive relationship with ourselves, which is foundational to overall well-being.

To illustrate the tangible benefits, consider the widespread research on mindfulness-based stress reduction (MBSR) programs. These programs, which often involve guided meditation, body awareness, and mindful movement, have demonstrated significant effectiveness in reducing symptoms of anxiety, depression, and chronic pain. Participants often report improved sleep, increased focus, and a greater overall sense of well-being. These outcomes are not a result of magical thinking, but rather the direct consequence of rewiring the brain's response to stress and cultivating a more balanced and engaged relationship with one's internal and external experiences. The principles of mindful living are not abstract concepts; they are practical tools that can be learned and applied to create a more fulfilling and resilient life. By consciously choosing to be present, we begin to inhabit our lives more fully, transforming ordinary moments into opportunities for peace, connection, and genuine happiness. It is an invitation to awaken to the richness that already exists within and around us, to savor the present, and to build a life that is truly lived, not merely experienced in passing.

Building Resilience Through Contentment

The journey toward personal happiness and well-being is significantly bolstered by the cultivation of contentment, a disposition that acts as a potent shield against life's inherent turbulence. While gratitude prompts us to appreciate what we possess, contentment allows us to truly inhabit that state of appreciation, fostering a deep-seated inner stability that renders us less vulnerable to the sting of disappointment and the pangs of envy. It is a quiet yet powerful acknowledgment of the present, a conscious decision to find peace and satisfaction in the 'enough' that already exists, rather than perpetually chasing after an elusive 'more'. This shift in focus from lack to abundance is not about resignation or complacency; rather, it is a strategic redirection of our mental and emotional resources towards appreciating and leveraging what we have, thereby building a robust foundation of resilience.

Individuals who actively practice contentment often demonstrate a remarkable capacity to navigate adversity with grace and fortitude. When faced with setbacks, their internal compass points towards their existing strengths and resources, rather than dwelling on what has been lost or what is missing. This positive orientation allows them to approach challenges not as insurmountable obstacles, but as opportunities to adapt and grow. Consider the individual who experiences a job loss. While the initial shock and disappointment are natural, a contented mindset would prompt them to acknowledge the skills and experience they have gained, the support network they can rely on, and the potential for new avenues to open up. Instead of succumbing to despair or self-pity, they are more likely to engage in proactive problem-solving, drawing on their existing strengths to craft a plan for their next steps. This proactive stance is a direct consequence of their focus on what they have, which fuels a sense of agency and self-efficacy, enabling them to bounce back from the disruption with greater speed and a more optimistic outlook.

This inherent stability that contentment provides is crucial in preventing external circumstances from dictating our internal state. When our sense of satisfaction is tied to external achievements, possessions, or the opinions of others, we become inherently fragile. The inevitable fluctuations in these external factors can then trigger significant emotional distress. Contentment, however, anchors our sense of well-being within ourselves. It is the understanding that while external circumstances may change, our capacity for peace and happiness can remain constant, rooted in our ability to appreciate our present reality. This internal anchoring makes us less susceptible to the anxieties and stresses that plague those who are constantly seeking validation or fulfillment outside themselves. The relentless pursuit of more can become an endless cycle, leaving individuals feeling perpetually unfulfilled. Contentment offers a way to break this cycle, to recognize that true wealth lies not in accumulation, but in appreciation.

Furthermore, contentment fosters a more balanced and realistic perspective on life. It encourages us to accept that life is a mix of positive and negative experiences, successes and failures, joys and sorrows. Rather than striving for a utopian existence devoid of challenges, a contented person understands that difficulties are an integral part of the human journey. This acceptance reduces the emotional burden of striving for an unattainable ideal and allows for a more genuine and compassionate engagement with reality. When we are less preoccupied with wishing things were different, we are more present to the reality of what *is*.

This presence, in turn, allows us to address challenges more effectively. For instance, instead of lamenting a perceived personal failing, a contented individual might acknowledge it as a learning experience, focusing on how they can improve moving forward without being overly self-critical. This mindset is a powerful driver of emotional recovery, enabling a quicker return to equilibrium after experiencing adversity.

The practice of contentment is not a passive state; it is an active engagement with life, characterized by a conscious effort to appreciate the good, accept the imperfect, and find meaning in the ordinary. This active engagement manifests in a variety of ways. For example, in relationships, contentment allows us to appreciate our loved ones for who they are, rather than constantly focusing on their perceived flaws or unmet expectations. This appreciation deepens connection and fosters a more harmonious environment. When we are content with our relationships, we are less likely to engage in passive-aggressive behaviors or harbor unspoken resentments. Instead, we are more inclined to communicate openly and with kindness, recognizing the value of the bond we share. This, in turn, strengthens the relationship and provides a reliable source of emotional support during difficult times.

Moreover, contentment has a profound impact on our physical health. Chronic stress, often fueled by dissatisfaction and a sense of lack, can have detrimental effects on the body, contributing to a host of health problems. By reducing stress and fostering a more positive emotional state, contentment can lead to improved sleep, a stronger immune system, and a greater sense of overall vitality. When we are not constantly agitated by unmet desires or anxieties about the future, our bodies can enter a state of greater ease and restoration. This is not to say that contentment eliminates all stressors, but rather that it equips us with a more resilient internal state to manage them effectively, thereby mitigating their negative impact on our physical well-being.

The cultivation of contentment is a skill that can be developed and strengthened over time through consistent practice. One effective strategy is to regularly engage in gratitude practices, as discussed previously. By consciously acknowledging and appreciating the good things in our lives, however small, we reinforce the habit of focusing on abundance rather than scarcity. Another key practice is mindfulness, which allows us to be fully present in the moment and appreciate the richness of everyday experiences. When we are mindful, we can savor the simple pleasures – the warmth of the sun on our skin, the taste of a good meal, the sound of laughter – which often go unnoticed when our minds are preoccupied with worries or desires. These moments of mindful appreciation, when accumulated, create a powerful counter-narrative to feelings of dissatisfaction.

Reframing our thoughts is also a crucial component of building contentment. This involves consciously challenging negative or scarcity-based thinking patterns. For instance, if a thought arises such as "I'll never be happy until I achieve X," it can be reframed to "I am capable of finding happiness in the present moment, and achieving X would be a bonus." This simple shift in perspective can significantly alter our emotional response to circumstances. It's about recognizing that happiness is not a destination to be reached after a series of accomplishments, but a state of being that can be cultivated and experienced here and now. This internal shift allows us to engage with life's journey with a greater sense of peace and fulfillment, rather than being perpetually caught in the "if only" mindset.

The ability to find contentment also influences our approach to goals and ambitions. Instead of pursuing goals out of a sense of inadequacy or a desperate need to prove something, contented individuals are more likely to pursue them from a place of genuine interest and desire for growth. This makes the pursuit itself more enjoyable and less fraught with anxiety. Even if the ultimate goal is not achieved, the process of working towards it can still be fulfilling because the individual's sense of worth is not solely dependent on the outcome. This detachment from the outcome, while still maintaining commitment to the effort, is a hallmark of resilient individuals who can weather disappointments without compromising their inner peace.

Consider the practice of setting realistic expectations. Life is rarely a perfect upward trajectory. There will be plateaus, dips, and unexpected detours. By accepting this reality and setting expectations that are grounded in this understanding, we are less likely to experience the sharp disappointment that comes from unmet idealistic hopes. This doesn't mean lowering our aspirations, but rather tempering them with a healthy dose of realism. For example, expecting a project to encounter some challenges is far more conducive to resilience than expecting a seamless and effortless completion. When challenges inevitably arise, a realistic expectation allows for a calmer, more problem-solving-oriented response, rather than an emotional meltdown.

Furthermore, the practice of contentment cultivates a sense of abundance, which is a powerful antidote to the scarcity mindset that often fuels anxiety and unhappiness. When we are focused on what we lack, our minds are perpetually scanning for deficiencies. Conversely, when we focus on what we have – our health, our relationships, our skills, the simple comforts of daily life – our perception shifts. We begin to see the wealth that already surrounds us. This shift in perception is not about denying the existence of difficulties or the need for improvement, but about consciously choosing where to direct our attention. This redirection of focus can profoundly impact our overall well-being and our ability to cope with adversity.

The interplay between contentment and resilience is a virtuous cycle. As we cultivate contentment, we build our resilience.

And as we experience success in navigating challenges with resilience, our sense of contentment deepens.

This symbiotic relationship means that each effort to foster one practice reinforces the other, creating a powerful momentum towards greater personal happiness and well-being. It is about recognizing that the most enduring forms of happiness are not derived from constant external validation or the acquisition of more, but from the internal cultivation of peace, appreciation, and acceptance. Contentment, therefore, is not merely a pleasant emotional state; it is a strategic approach to life that builds a robust and enduring capacity to thrive amidst the inevitable complexities and uncertainties of our existence. It is the quiet strength that allows us to stand firm when the winds of change blow, knowing that even if circumstances shift, our inner foundation remains secure, built upon the solid ground of what we already possess and deeply appreciate. This internal bedrock of contentment is what truly empowers us to face life's storms not with fear, but with a quiet confidence and an unwavering spirit.

The Role of Self-Care in Sustainable Happiness

The cultivation of personal happiness and well-being, as we have explored, is an ongoing journey, not a destination. It is a dynamic process that requires conscious effort and strategic implementation. Within this framework, the foundational pillar that underpins our ability to not only achieve but sustain happiness is the practice of self-care. This is not a tangential aspect of well-being, but rather its very bedrock, enabling us to navigate life's complexities with grace, resilience, and an enduring sense of fulfillment. Without a robust commitment to self-care, any happiness we achieve is likely to be fragile, susceptible to the inevitable storms of life. It is the essential fuel that powers our capacity for joy, our ability to connect with others, and our overall effectiveness in the world.

To truly understand the power of self-care, it is crucial to define it expansively. It is far more than indulging in occasional treats or taking a day off. Self-care encompasses a holistic approach to nurturing our physical, emotional, and mental health. Physically, it means providing our bodies with the fundamental nourishment they require to function optimally. This includes ensuring we obtain adequate sleep, which is critical for cognitive function, emotional regulation, and physical restoration. It involves making conscious choices about what we eat, opting for foods that energize us rather than deplete us. Regular physical activity, tailored to our individual needs and preferences, is also a non-negotiable component, releasing endorphins, reducing stress hormones, and improving our overall physical resilience. These practices are not about achieving a particular aesthetic, but about honoring our bodies as the vessels that carry us through life, ensuring they are strong, healthy, and capable.

Beyond the physical, self-care is deeply intertwined with our emotional landscape. It involves acknowledging, understanding, and managing our emotions in healthy ways. This might mean setting boundaries in relationships, learning to say no to requests that would overextend us, or creating space for activities that bring us genuine joy and emotional replenishment. Emotional self-care also entails processing difficult feelings, perhaps through journaling, talking with a trusted friend or therapist, or engaging in creative expression. It is about cultivating an inner environment where emotions are not suppressed or ignored, but met with compassion and understanding. This allows us to move through challenges without becoming overwhelmed, fostering a greater sense of emotional equilibrium and a more positive outlook on life.

Equally vital is the mental dimension of self-care. In our fast-paced, information-saturated world, our minds are constantly bombarded with stimuli. Mental self-care involves actively managing this influx, protecting our cognitive resources, and engaging in activities that stimulate our intellect and creativity in positive ways. This can include practicing mindfulness or meditation to quiet the mental chatter, engaging in learning new skills or pursuing intellectually stimulating hobbies, or simply taking breaks from demanding tasks to allow our minds to rest and recharge. It is about being intentional with our thoughts, challenging negative self-talk, and cultivating a mindset that is both realistic and optimistic. Prioritizing mental self-care is essential for maintaining focus, enhancing problem-solving abilities, and preventing burnout.

The concept of self-care has, unfortunately, become mired in misconceptions. It is often mistakenly viewed as a selfish indulgence, a luxury reserved for those with ample free time, or a sign of weakness. This perception is not only inaccurate but actively detrimental to our well-being. In reality, self-care is not selfish; it is a prerequisite for effective engagement with the world and with others. Imagine trying to pour from an empty cup. Without tending to our own needs, we quickly deplete our resources, leaving us unable to offer our best selves to our relationships, our work, or our communities. Prioritizing self-care is akin to the oxygen mask instruction on an airplane: you must secure your own mask before assisting others. It is a responsible and necessary act that enables us to be more present, more effective, and ultimately, more generous with our time, energy, and love.

Furthermore, reframing self-care as a vital investment rather than an indulgence is crucial for its consistent practice. Just as a business invests in its employees and infrastructure to ensure long-term success, we must invest in our own well-being to foster sustainable happiness and achieve our goals. This investment yields significant returns: increased energy, improved mood, enhanced resilience, greater creativity, and a deeper sense of overall satisfaction with life. When we feel good, both physically and mentally, we are better equipped to handle stress, solve problems, and contribute positively to the lives of those around us. The energy and clarity gained from consistent self-care allow us to be more effective in our professional lives, more engaged in our personal relationships, and more capable of facing challenges with a positive and proactive attitude.

The journey of cultivating self-care is inherently personal, and what constitutes effective self-care varies greatly from one individual to another. What one person finds restorative; another might find draining. Therefore, a key aspect of this practice is self-awareness and experimentation. It involves paying attention to what activities, habits, and environments genuinely nourish you, and what tends to deplete your energy or heighten your stress levels. For some, self-care might look like a quiet morning with a book and a cup of tea. For others, it could be a vigorous workout, a creative pursuit like painting or playing music, spending time in nature, or connecting with loved ones. The common thread is that these activities are chosen consciously and deliberately for their positive impact on your overall well-being. It is about understanding your unique needs and responding to them with intention and care.

To integrate self-care into your life more effectively, consider it through the lens of intentionality. Instead of letting self-care happen by chance, plan for it. Schedule time for activities that recharge you, just as you would schedule important appointments or work meetings. Start small; even five or ten minutes dedicated to a calming activity can make a difference. Perhaps it's a short meditation, a few deep breaths, or a brief walk around the block. As these small practices become habitual, you can gradually increase the time and incorporate a wider range of self-care activities. The goal is not to add more stress to your life by creating an overwhelming to-do list, but to weave moments of nourishment into the fabric of your daily routine.

Moreover, self-care is not a one-time fix; it is a continuous practice. Life is dynamic, and our needs will change over time. What serves as effective self-care during a period of high stress might differ from what we need during a more relaxed phase. Therefore, it is essential to periodically reassess your self-care routine and make adjustments as needed. Be adaptable and compassionate with yourself. There will be days when sticking to your self-care plan is challenging, perhaps due to unexpected demands or simply feeling unmotivated. On such days, the most beneficial form of self-care might be to acknowledge these feelings without judgment and to do the best you can, even if it's just a small act of kindness towards yourself.

The connection between self-care and sustainable happiness is profound and symbiotic. When we consistently prioritize our well-being, we build a stronger internal foundation. This foundation acts as a buffer against life's inevitable stressors, enabling us to bounce back more effectively from setbacks. Think of it as building emotional and physical resilience. The more we invest in our self-care, the greater our capacity becomes to manage challenges, maintain a positive outlook, and experience joy, even amidst adversity. Happiness derived from a place of self-neglect is often fleeting and superficial. True, lasting happiness, however, is cultivated from a place of self-nurturing and self-respect. It is the kind of happiness that radiates from within, enriching our own lives and positively influencing those around us.

In essence, self-care is the active, ongoing commitment to fostering your own physical, emotional, and mental well-being. It is a conscious choice to honor your needs, protect your energy, and engage in activities that replenish and restore you. By embracing self-care not as a luxury but as a necessity, you lay the groundwork for a life characterized by sustained happiness, greater resilience, and a deeper capacity to connect with and contribute to the world around you. It is the silent strength that empowers you to live a fuller, more vibrant, and more meaningful life. Prioritizing your own well-being is not just about personal benefit; it is about creating the capacity to be truly present and effective in all areas of your life, making you a more valuable and contributing member of your family, your community, and the wider world. The commitment to self-care is, therefore, a commitment to living your best life, authentically and sustainably.

Chapter 4: Fostering a More Peaceful and Loving Society

The journey towards a more peaceful and loving society is intricate, and at its very core lies a quality that transcends mere politeness or superficial understanding: empathy. If self-care is the bedrock of individual well-being, then empathy is the bedrock of genuine human connection. It is the invisible thread that binds us, allowing us to perceive the world not just through our own eyes, but through the eyes of another. This ability to step outside our own experience and into the emotional and cognitive landscape of another person is not just a desirable trait; it is a fundamental requirement for bridging divides, dissolving conflict, and fostering a society that truly cares for its members. Without empathy, our interactions remain shallow, our understanding incomplete, and our potential for collective flourishing severely limited.

Empathy is the profound ability to understand and share the feelings of another. It's about recognizing the humanity in someone else, even when their experiences, beliefs, or circumstances are vastly different from our own.

This isn't about agreeing with them, condoning their actions, or even necessarily liking them. Rather, it is about acknowledging their internal world, their joys, their sorrows, their fears, and their hopes, as if they were our own. It's a form of emotional resonance, a deep listening that goes beyond the spoken words to grasp the unspoken emotions that fuel them. When we practice empathy, we are essentially saying, "*I* may not fully understand your situation, but *I* can feel with you, and *I* acknowledge your experience as valid."

Consider the common experience of misunderstanding. How often do disagreements escalate not because of fundamental differences in principle, but because each party feels unheard and unacknowledged? We become entrenched in our own perspective, convinced of our own righteousness, and unable to penetrate the defensive walls that rise around us. Empathy offers a way through this. When we consciously try to understand the perspective of someone with whom we disagree, we begin to dismantle those walls. This might involve actively listening to their arguments without formulating a rebuttal in our head, asking clarifying questions that seek to understand their motivations and feelings, and trying to identify the underlying needs or values that drive their position.

For instance, imagine a community meeting where two groups are at odds over a local development project. One group might be primarily concerned with economic growth and job creation, while the other prioritizes environmental preservation and the protection of natural spaces. Without empathy, this debate can quickly devolve into accusations and animosity. However, if members from both sides make an effort to understand the other's core concerns – the anxieties about job loss versus the deep-seated fear of irreversible ecological damage – a path towards compromise might emerge. Empathy allows us to see that both groups are motivated by legitimate concerns for the well-being of their community, even if their proposed solutions differ. It shifts the focus from the familiar "us versus them" to a shared exploration of how to meet the needs of all stakeholders.

The psychological underpinnings of empathy are fascinating. Neuroscience reveals that when we witness another person experiencing an emotion, similar neural pathways in our own brains can become activated. This "mirroring" is a biological basis for our capacity to feel what others feel. However, empathy is not purely an automatic, involuntary response. It is also a skill that can be consciously cultivated and strengthened. It requires intention, practice, and a willingness to be vulnerable. This is where the connection to self-care becomes evident. Just as we learned that tending to our own needs makes us more capable of engaging with the world, developing our empathetic capacity requires an inner state of readiness. When we are emotionally regulated and have a strong sense of our own worth, we are less likely to feel threatened by others' perspectives and more open to understanding them.

Cultivating empathy involves several key practices. The first is active listening. This means more than just hearing the words; it involves paying full attention to the speaker, both verbally and non-verbally. It means observing their tone of voice, their body language, and the emotions that might be conveyed through these channels. It involves resisting the urge to interrupt, to judge, or to impose our own narrative. Instead, we focus on understanding the speaker's message in its entirety. Paraphrasing what we hear – "So, if I understand correctly, you're feeling frustrated because..." – can be a powerful tool for ensuring comprehension and demonstrating that we are truly engaged.

Another crucial element is perspective-taking. This is the cognitive aspect of empathy, where we consciously try to imagine ourselves in the other person's situation. What might be driving their behavior? What are their underlying beliefs, values, and fears? This requires us to suspend our own assumptions and biases and to approach the situation with curiosity rather than judgment. It's about asking, "What would it feel like to be them, in this moment?" This mental exercise can unlock a profound understanding of motivations that might otherwise seem inexplicable or even malicious.

Relatability plays a significant role here. While we may not have experienced the exact same circumstances as another person, we all share fundamental human emotions and needs.

We have all felt fear, disappointment, joy, love, and loss. By tapping into these shared human experiences, we can find common ground and build bridges of understanding. Recognizing that the person we disagree with also experiences vulnerability, hopes for their children, and fears for their future can be a powerful catalyst for empathy. It reminds us of our shared humanity, which often gets obscured by superficial differences.

Expressing empathy is as important as cultivating it. Simply understanding another person's feelings is not enough; we must also convey that understanding to them. This can be done through verbal affirmations, such as saying, "I can see why you would feel that way," or "That sounds incredibly difficult." It can also be done through non-verbal cues, like maintaining eye contact, nodding in agreement, or offering a comforting gesture if appropriate. When people feel that their emotions are recognized and validated, it creates a sense of safety and trust, which is essential for any meaningful connection.

The impact of empathy extends far beyond individual relationships. It is the very foundation upon which a more peaceful and loving society can be built. When empathy is widespread, it influences our institutions, our policies, and our collective responses to challenges. Consider how societies respond to crises, whether natural disasters, economic downturns, or social injustices. A society rich in empathy will naturally gravitate towards supporting those most affected, seeking equitable solutions, and fostering a sense of collective responsibility. Conversely, a society lacking in empathy is prone to division, marginalization, and the perpetuation of suffering.

In the realm of conflict resolution, empathy is not a sign of weakness but a strategic necessity. When parties in a dispute can empathize with each other's positions, they are far more likely to find common ground and de-escalate tensions. This applies to everything from interpersonal disputes to international relations. Diplomatic efforts, for example, are often most effective when they are grounded in a deep understanding of the other nation's history, culture, fears, and aspirations. Ignoring or dismissing these factors often leads to miscalculations and prolonged conflict.

Furthermore, empathy is a powerful antidote to prejudice and discrimination. Prejudice often stems from a lack of understanding and an inability to see individuals as more than stereotypes. By actively seeking to understand the experiences of people from different backgrounds, cultures, or identities, we can challenge our own biases and dismantle the foundations of discrimination. When we recognize the humanity and shared experiences of those who are different from us, the urge to other them diminishes, and the capacity for acceptance and inclusion grows. This process requires a conscious effort to learn, to listen, and to engage with narratives that might challenge our existing worldview. It means actively seeking out diverse perspectives, reading books by Dr. *A.* Romani, and other authors from different backgrounds, watching films that explore different lived experiences, and engaging in respectful conversations with people whose lives are different from our own.

The challenge, of course, is that cultivating empathy in a world that often rewards competition and self-interest can be difficult. There are times when our own emotional reserves are depleted, and extending empathy to others feels like an impossible task. This is precisely why the connection to self-care is so vital. When we are tending to our own well-being, we are better equipped to extend our capacity for care outwards. A person who is emotionally depleted, stressed, or overwhelmed is less likely to have the mental and emotional bandwidth to engage empathetically with others. Conversely, someone who is rested, resourced, and emotionally stable is more capable of offering understanding and compassion.

Moreover, our societal structures and cultural narratives can either foster or hinder empathy. Media portrayals, political rhetoric, and educational systems all play a role in shaping our capacity to connect with one another. When society emphasizes competition over cooperation, individual success over collective well-being, or demonizes opposing viewpoints, it creates an environment where empathy struggles to thrive. Conversely, societies that celebrate collaboration, promote understanding, and provide platforms for diverse voices to be heard are more likely to cultivate a widespread sense of empathy.

Therefore, fostering empathy is not just an individual responsibility; it is also a societal imperative. It requires a conscious effort to create environments that encourage understanding and connection. This can include promoting dialogue across differences, implementing educational programs that teach emotional intelligence and perspective-taking, and encouraging media that humanizes diverse groups rather than perpetuating stereotypes.

The process of developing empathy is ongoing. It's a muscle that needs to be exercised regularly. It means making conscious choices in our daily interactions: to pause before reacting, to listen more than we speak, to ask questions that seek understanding, and to look for the shared humanity in every person we encounter. It means being willing to be wrong, to learn, and to grow. It means recognizing that true connection is built not on shared opinions, but on shared understanding and mutual respect for the inherent dignity of each individual. By embracing empathy as the cornerstone of our interactions, we begin to weave a stronger, more compassionate social fabric, moving us closer to the peaceful and loving society we aspire to create. It is in this willingness to truly see and feel with another that the seeds of profound social change are sown.

Compassion in Action Beyond Sympathy

The preceding exploration has illuminated empathy as the foundational understanding and sharing of another's feelings – the crucial ability to step into their shoes and acknowledge their lived experience. Yet, while empathy opens the door to connection, it is compassion that propels us forward, transforming understanding into a force for positive change. Compassion is empathy with a vital addition: a deep-seated desire to alleviate suffering and a proactive commitment to action. It is not merely feeling *for* someone, but feeling *with* them and then being moved to *do* something about it. This distinction is critical. Sympathy can be a passive acknowledgement of another's distress, a feeling of pity from a distance. Empathy deepens this, allowing us to share in their emotional reality. Compassion, however, ignites a desire to act, to offer support, to mend, to heal, and to contribute to a more just and humane world. It's the bridge between recognizing suffering and actively working to reduce it.

Consider the ripple effect of a single compassionate act. A neighbor sees an elderly person struggling to carry groceries and offers to help. This is more than just empathy; it's compassion in action. The neighbor understands the difficulty and the potential strain, and they choose to intervene, to lighten the load, both literally and figuratively. This small act can transform the recipient's day, alleviating physical discomfort and offering a powerful message of care and connection. For the neighbor, it's an opportunity to practice their capacity for kindness and to strengthen community bonds. These seemingly small moments are the building blocks of a more caring society. They demonstrate that we are not isolated islands but interconnected beings whose well-being is intertwined.

The beauty of compassion lies in its versatility; it manifests in countless ways, adaptable to individual circumstances and capacities. It doesn't always require grand gestures or significant resources. Often, the most impactful expressions of compassion are woven into the fabric of our daily lives. It can be the attentive ear offered to a friend grappling with a difficult decision, providing a non-judgmental space for them to process their thoughts and emotions. It can be the patient explanation given to a child struggling with a concept, recognizing their frustration and offering guidance with understanding. It can be the willingness to step in and help a colleague who is overwhelmed, sharing the burden and demonstrating solidarity. These acts, though perhaps quiet and personal, are potent expressions of our shared humanity.

In families, compassion acts as a vital lubricant, smoothing over the inevitable friction of close living. When a parent patiently guides a child through a tantrum, acknowledging their big feelings while setting necessary boundaries, that is compassion. When siblings offer support to one another during times of stress or disappointment, sharing a burden or offering encouragement, that is compassion. It's about understanding that each family member is navigating their own challenges and choosing to respond with care rather than exasperation or indifference. This creates an environment of safety and trust, where vulnerability is met with understanding, fostering deeper bonds and resilience within the family unit.

Beyond the immediate family, compassion extends outwards to our communities. Think of the volunteers who dedicate their time to local shelters, offering comfort and practical assistance to those experiencing homelessness or hardship. Their empathy allows them to grasp the profound difficulties faced by these individuals, and their compassion motivates them to act, providing meals, clothing, or simply a listening ear. This is not about pity; it's about recognizing the inherent dignity of every person and taking tangible steps to alleviate suffering. Consider also the individuals who organize food drives, collect donations for disaster relief, or mentor at-risk youth. These are all manifestations of compassion, translating a deep concern for others into organized efforts that create tangible positive change.

The act of donating to a cause we believe in, whether it's supporting medical research, environmental protection, or social justice initiatives, is another powerful expression of compassion. It's an acknowledgement that there are problems in the world that extend beyond our immediate personal lives, and a willingness to contribute our resources, however modest, to address them.

This financial or material support allows organizations to continue their work, extending care and aid to a wider population. It's a way of extending our empathetic reach, recognizing that the well-being of others, even strangers, matters.

Furthermore, compassion can be a powerful force in the workplace. A manager who understands the challenges an employee is facing outside of work and offers flexibility or support is demonstrating compassion. Colleagues who collaborate effectively, offering help and sharing credit, rather than engaging in cutthroat competition, are fostering a compassionate work environment. This not only improves morale and productivity but also creates a more humane and supportive atmosphere where individuals feel valued and understood. When empathy and compassion are present in professional settings, it shifts the focus from purely transactional relationships to more collaborative and supportive ones.

One of the most profound ways compassion can be enacted is through forgiveness and understanding, particularly in situations of conflict or harm. While empathy allows us to understand the motivations or circumstances that might have led to hurtful actions, compassion empowers us to move beyond resentment and to seek reconciliation or at least a reduction in the intensity of the conflict. This doesn't mean excusing harmful behavior or ignoring injustice. Instead, it involves recognizing the humanity even in those who have erred, understanding that they too are fallible beings, and choosing to respond with a desire for healing rather than retribution. This is exceptionally challenging, but it is in these difficult moments that compassion's transformative power is most evident.

Consider the restorative justice movements that are gaining traction in various communities. These approaches often prioritize dialogue and understanding between those who have caused harm and those who have been harmed, aiming for accountability, healing, and reintegration rather than solely punishment. The underlying principle is rooted in compassion – a belief that even those who have committed offenses deserve a chance to understand the impact of their actions and to contribute to repair, and that victims deserve to have their voices heard and their suffering acknowledged in a way that promotes healing. This requires immense courage and vulnerability from all parties involved, but the potential for genuine transformation and reconciliation is immense.

Education also plays a crucial role in fostering compassion. When children are taught about emotional intelligence, empathy, and the importance of kindness from an early age, they are more likely to grow into adults who act with compassion. Schools that incorporate service-learning projects, encourage volunteerism, and actively promote a culture of care create fertile ground for compassion to flourish. These experiences provide practical opportunities for students to translate their understanding of others' needs into meaningful action, shaping their values and their behavior.

The media we consume also influences our capacity for compassion. Stories that highlight acts of kindness, resilience, and the struggles of marginalized communities can open our hearts and minds, fostering a greater sense of connection and a desire to help. Conversely, media that sensationalizes conflict, perpetuates stereotypes, or focuses solely on individualistic narratives can inadvertently erode our compassionate instincts. Being mindful of the media we engage with and seeking out stories that humanize others is an active way to cultivate our compassionate outlook.

It's important to acknowledge that practicing compassion is not always easy. There will be times when we feel drained, overwhelmed, or even resentful, particularly when faced with persistent injustice or repeated harm. It is in these moments that the connection between self-care and compassion becomes undeniably clear. Just as we learned that empathy requires a certain inner equilibrium, compassionate action is more sustainable when we are not depleted ourselves. Prioritizing our own physical, emotional, and mental well-being is not selfish; it is essential for enabling us to effectively extend care to others. A burned-out caregiver cannot offer effective support. Therefore, recognizing our limits, setting healthy boundaries, and engaging in activities that replenish our energy are crucial for sustained compassionate engagement.

Moreover, the societal context in which we live plays a significant role in either nurturing or inhibiting compassion. Societies that emphasize competition, individualism, and a zero-sum mentality can make it more challenging to prioritize collective well-being and altruistic action. Conversely, cultures that celebrate cooperation, interdependence, and mutual support provide a more fertile ground for compassion to thrive. We can actively work to foster more compassionate environments in our own spheres of influence, whether that's in our families, workplaces, or communities, by modeling compassionate behavior, speaking out against injustice, and supporting initiatives that promote connection and care.

Ultimately, becoming agents of compassion is about making conscious choices every day. It's about looking for opportunities to make a positive difference, however small. It might be offering a compliment, holding a door, offering a helping hand, or simply listening with genuine presence. These are not trivial acts. They are the threads that weave a stronger, more resilient, and more loving social fabric. They demonstrate that we are not passive observers of suffering but active participants in creating a world where kindness and care are paramount. By moving beyond passive sympathy and embracing active compassion, we unlock our potential to be true healers, builders, and sources of light in the world, contributing to a society that is not only more peaceful but profoundly more loving. It's about recognizing that every interaction is an opportunity to offer a piece of our humanity, to extend a hand of support, and to affirm the inherent worth of every soul we encounter, thereby shaping a collective future where care is not an exception, but the norm.

Mutual Respect in a Diverse World

In our journey toward a more peaceful and loving society, having explored the foundational role of empathy and the action-oriented nature of compassion, we now turn our attention to a pillar of interconnectedness that is indispensable in a world increasingly defined by its multifaceted tapestry of human experience: mutual respect. As our communities become more vibrant mosaics of cultures, traditions, beliefs, and backgrounds, the ability to not just coexist but to genuinely appreciate and value one another becomes paramount. This isn't merely about avoiding conflict; it is about actively building bridges of understanding and fostering an environment where every individual feels seen, heard, and inherently worthy of consideration.

The essence of mutual respect lies in acknowledging the intrinsic dignity and worth of every human being, irrespective of their differences. It's a recognition that while our paths may diverge, our shared humanity binds us. This understanding transcends mere tolerance, which can often imply a reluctant acceptance of something one dislikes. Instead, mutual respect calls for a deeper engagement, a willingness to learn, and an active appreciation for the unique perspectives and experiences that each person brings to the collective human narrative. When we approach interactions with a spirit of respect, we create an atmosphere conducive to dialogue, collaboration, and genuine connection.

Navigating the complexities of a diverse world requires a conscious and consistent effort to cultivate this respect. It begins with an honest self-assessment of our own biases, assumptions, and preconceived notions. We all carry mental frameworks shaped by our upbringing, environment, and personal experiences, which can inadvertently lead us to judge or devalue those who are different from us. Recognizing these internal landscapes is the first step towards dismantling them. It involves a commitment to curiosity over judgment, to seeking understanding rather than validation of our own viewpoints.

One of the most powerful avenues for fostering mutual respect is through engaging in respectful dialogue. This means creating safe spaces where individuals feel empowered to express their thoughts, feelings, and beliefs without fear of ridicule or dismissal. It requires active listening – not just waiting for our turn to speak, but truly endeavoring to grasp the speaker's meaning, their underlying emotions, and their unique frame of reference. When we listen with the intent to understand, rather than to refute, we open ourselves to the possibility of learning and growth, and we signal to the other person that their voice matters.

Consider the myriad ways in which cultural differences can manifest. From variations in communication styles, such as directness versus indirectness, to differing norms around personal space, punctuality, or expressions of emotion, these variations can, if not approached with respect, lead to misunderstandings and unintended offense. For instance, a culture that values direct communication might perceive indirectness as evasiveness or dishonesty, while a culture that favors indirectness might view directness as aggressive or rude. By understanding these underlying cultural values and approaching interactions with an open mind, we can navigate these differences with grace, assuming positive intent until proven otherwise. This requires a willingness to ask clarifying questions rather than making assumptions, and to express our own needs and perspectives respectfully.

The same principle applies to differences in beliefs, whether religious, political, or philosophical. In a pluralistic society, encountering viewpoints that diverge from our own is not an anomaly; it is an expectation. Mutual respect dictates that we engage with these differences constructively. This doesn't necessitate agreement, but it does demand that we acknowledge the right of others to hold their beliefs and to express them. It means engaging in debate and discussion with civility, focusing on the substance of ideas rather than resorting to personal attacks or generalizations. It's about recognizing that differing beliefs often stem from deeply held values and life experiences, and that challenging someone's beliefs is not the same as disrespecting their personhood.

Moreover, mutual respect extends to appreciating the unique contributions that individuals from all walks of life bring to our communities. The elderly offer wisdom gleaned from years of experience; youth bring fresh perspectives and innovative ideas; individuals from different socio-economic backgrounds provide insights into varied realities; people with disabilities demonstrate resilience and unique problem-solving skills; those from diverse ethnic and racial groups enrich our cultural landscape with their traditions, arts, and culinary heritage. When we actively seek out and value these diverse contributions, we create a richer, more dynamic, and more resilient society. This is not about tokenism; it is about genuine recognition and integration.

The challenge of maintaining mutual respect is amplified in situations of historical injustice or ongoing social inequalities. In such contexts, simply calling for respect can feel insufficient if it doesn't acknowledge the systemic barriers and experiences of marginalization that certain groups have faced. True mutual respect in these situations involves a willingness to listen to and learn from the lived experiences of those who have been historically disadvantaged, to acknowledge past wrongs, and to actively work towards creating a more equitable future. It means understanding that for some, the path to feeling respected is intertwined with the dismantling of oppressive structures and the affirmation of their inherent worth and rights.

Fostering mutual respect is also an ongoing, active process. It requires conscious effort in our daily interactions, from the casual conversations with neighbors to the formal discussions in workplaces or public forums. It means choosing our words carefully, being mindful of our body language, and consistently demonstrating a commitment to fairness and consideration. When we witness disrespect, whether it's subtle microaggressions or overt acts of prejudice, it is important, where it is safe and appropriate to do so, to speak up or to offer support to those who are being targeted. This collective action reinforces the norm of respect and signals that such behavior is unacceptable.

In the digital age, where communication often occurs through screens, the challenge of maintaining mutual respect can be particularly acute. The anonymity or perceived distance of online interactions can sometimes embolden individuals to express themselves in ways they would never consider in face-to-face encounters. Online platforms can become breeding grounds for vitriol, misinformation, and personal attacks. Cultivating mutual respect online requires a conscious decision to treat others with the same courtesy and consideration we would offer in person. It means engaging in constructive discourse, fact-checking information before sharing it, and refraining from personal attacks or inflammatory language. It also involves reporting and challenging hateful or disrespectful content when we encounter it.

Building a society grounded in mutual respect also involves educating future generations. Schools and families have a crucial role to play in teaching children about diversity, inclusion, and the importance of treating everyone with dignity. This education should go beyond simply stating that differences exist; it should actively explore the richness that diversity brings and equip children with the skills to communicate effectively and respectfully across differences. Programs that promote cross-cultural understanding, empathy-building exercises, and opportunities for collaboration among diverse groups of young people can lay a strong foundation for a future society that embodies mutual respect.

Furthermore, leadership at all levels – in government, business, communities, and families – plays a critical role in setting the tone for mutual respect. Leaders who model respectful behavior, who champion diversity and inclusion, and who actively work to bridge divides can create a powerful ripple effect throughout society. When leaders demonstrate a genuine commitment to valuing all individuals, it empowers others to do the same. Conversely, leaders who engage in divisive rhetoric or who fail to condemn disrespect and prejudice inadvertently sanction such behaviors.

Ultimately, mutual respect is not a passive state but an active practice, a continuous choice to engage with others in a way that honors their humanity. It is the conscious decision to see the person behind the label, to understand the context behind the behavior, and to appreciate the value of every individual's unique journey. In a world brimming with differences, this commitment to mutual respect is not just a pathway to a more peaceful society; it is the very foundation upon which a truly loving and inclusive human community can be built, where every voice is heard, every person is valued, and every contribution is recognized as essential to our collective flourishing. It is the quiet strength that allows us to navigate our differences not as obstacles, but as opportunities for growth, connection, and a deeper understanding of ourselves and each other.

The Contribution of Contentment to Societal Harmony

The pursuit of a tranquil and compassionate society is inextricably linked to the cultivation of individual contentment. When individuals within a community find a sense of inner peace and satisfaction, it radiates outwards, fostering an environment that is less prone to the corrosive effects of envy, dissatisfaction, and relentless material accumulation. This shift from external acquisition to internal fulfillment fundamentally alters the dynamics of social interaction, paving the way for greater cooperation, mutual understanding, and a shared appreciation for collective well-being.

At its core, contentment is the quiet recognition that happiness and fulfillment are not contingent upon the acquisition of ever-increasing material possessions or status. It is a mindful appreciation for what one has, coupled with a realistic understanding of one's needs, rather than an insatiable yearning for more. This internal equilibrium acts as a powerful antidote to many of the societal ills that stem from a constant, often unfulfilled, desire for wealth and recognition. When individuals are content, they are less likely to be consumed by the comparative analysis of their own lives against those of others, a practice that often breeds resentment and envy. This reduction in corrosive emotions directly translates to less social friction, as the seeds of jealousy and covetousness, which so frequently lead to conflict and division, are effectively neutralized.

Consider the impact of financial prudence and mindful living on this cultivation of contentment. When individuals approach their finances with a sense of responsibility and moderation, avoiding the siren call of excessive debt and impulsive spending, they build a foundation of security that frees them from the anxieties of constant financial pressure. This freedom allows them to focus their energy on activities and relationships that genuinely nourish their spirit, rather than being perpetually caught in a hamster wheel of earning and spending. Similarly, mindful living, which involves paying attention to the present moment without judgment, helps individuals to detach from the incessant mental chatter of what they lack and to instead appreciate the richness of their current experience. This practice of presence allows for a deeper connection with oneself and with others, fostering a sense of gratitude that is the antithesis of dissatisfaction.

The ripple effect of individual contentment on societal harmony is profound. Contented individuals are inherently more inclined towards prosocial behaviors. When one's own needs are met and one's inner world is tranquil, there is a greater capacity to extend oneself to others. This manifests in various ways. For instance, a contented individual is more likely to volunteer their time and skills to community projects, not out of a sense of obligation or a need for external validation, but from a genuine desire to contribute to the common good. They are more likely to engage in acts of kindness, to offer support to those in need, and to participate actively in creating a more positive and supportive social fabric.

Think about the neighborhood dynamic. In communities where contentment is prevalent, you often find neighbors who are genuinely invested in each other's well-being. They might be the ones who offer to help an elderly neighbor with their groceries, who organize community clean-up days, or who simply make the effort to connect with those around them. These actions are not driven by a need to compete for social standing or to acquire status, but by a sense of shared humanity and a desire to foster a harmonious living environment. The absence of pervasive envy means that when a neighbor achieves a success, their contentment allows them to celebrate it genuinely, rather than feeling diminished by it. This shared joy and mutual support create a strong sense of belonging and collective identity.

Furthermore, contentment reduces the intensity of competitive drives that can become destructive when unchecked. In a society that often equates success with relentless ambition and material accumulation, the pressure to constantly outperform and outshine others can lead to a zero-sum mentality. This can manifest in workplaces, where collaboration may be sacrificed for individual gain, or in social circles, where comparison and competition can strain relationships. When individuals are content, this intense competitive pressure often dissipates. They are more secure in their own worth and less compelled to measure themselves against others. This allows for a greater emphasis on collaboration, as individuals recognize that shared success often leads to a more fulfilling outcome for everyone involved. Imagine a team working on a community garden. A contented team member is focused on the shared goal of growing food and beautifying the space, rather than worrying about who is weeding more or whose plot looks the best. This shared focus on a common, positive objective fosters camaraderie and makes the entire endeavor more enjoyable and productive.

The reduction in greed, another direct consequence of contentment, is crucial for societal harmony. Greed, the insatiable desire for more than one needs, can drive individuals to exploit others, engage in unethical practices, and disregard the well-being of the collective in their pursuit of personal gain. When people are content, their desires are more aligned with their genuine needs, and the powerful urge to hoard resources or to accumulate wealth beyond what is necessary diminishes significantly. This ethical grounding leads to more equitable interactions and a greater respect for shared resources. It means individuals are less likely to engage in behaviors that harm the environment or exploit vulnerable populations, as their focus shifts from unchecked acquisition to responsible stewardship and the well-being of the broader community.

Consider the impact of contentment on the political and economic spheres. A society composed of more contented individuals would likely experience less social unrest driven by economic disparity and perceived injustice. When people feel that their basic needs are met and that they have a reasonable opportunity to thrive, they are less susceptible to radicalization or to resentment towards those perceived as more fortunate. This doesn't imply a complete absence of desire for improvement or a passive acceptance of all circumstances, but rather a foundational stability that allows for constructive dialogue and problem-solving rather than outright conflict. Policies that promote equitable distribution of resources and opportunities, when embraced by a largely contented populace, are more likely to be seen as beneficial for all, fostering a sense of shared prosperity rather than division.

The contribution of contentment to societal harmony also extends to the realm of personal relationships. Envy and dissatisfaction can poison friendships and family bonds, leading to misunderstandings, arguments, and emotional distance. When individuals are content with their own lives, they are more present and appreciative in their interactions with loved ones. They are less likely to project their own insecurities onto others or to demand constant affirmation. This creates an environment where relationships can flourish based on genuine connection, mutual support, and shared joy, rather than being undermined by underlying feelings of inadequacy or competition. A contented parent, for example, is more likely to be patient and present with their children, fostering a secure and loving environment, rather than being consumed by anxieties about their own career trajectory or social standing.

Moreover, contented individuals often exhibit greater resilience in the face of adversity. Life inevitably presents challenges, and when individuals possess an inner wellspring of contentment, they are better equipped to navigate these difficulties without succumbing to despair or anger. This resilience not only benefits the individual but also contributes to the overall stability of the community. When a significant portion of the population can face setbacks with equanimity and a focus on constructive solutions, it creates a more stable and supportive social environment for everyone. They are less likely to become overwhelmed by negative emotions that can spill over into their interactions with others, maintaining a sense of balance and contributing positively to collective problem-solving.

The cultivation of contentment is not about advocating for stagnation or a lack of ambition. Rather, it is about redefining the nature of ambition itself, shifting it from a relentless pursuit of external validation and material gain to a focus on personal growth, meaningful contribution, and inner peace. When ambition is channeled through the lens of contentment, it becomes a force for positive creation and collective upliftment. Individuals may still strive for excellence, innovation, and progress, but their motivation stems from a desire to contribute to something larger than themselves and to find fulfillment in the process, rather than from a place of internal deficit or a need to prove their worth. This reframed ambition is inherently less damaging to societal harmony.

To foster this state of contentment on a larger scale, there needs to be a societal recognition of its value. This involves a cultural shift away from the pervasive narrative that equates happiness with consumption and towards one that celebrates inner fulfillment, meaningful relationships, and contribution to the common good. Educational systems can play a role by incorporating principles of mindfulness, gratitude, and financial literacy from an early age. Media and public discourse can also contribute by highlighting stories of individuals who find fulfillment outside the traditional metrics of wealth and status. Ultimately, the widespread cultivation of contentment is not merely a personal journey but a collective endeavor that holds the potential to significantly enhance societal harmony, reduce conflict, and pave the way for a more peaceful and loving world. It is the quiet strength that underpins genuine well-being, allowing individuals to thrive not at the expense of others, but in concert with them, fostering a flourishing society built on a foundation of inner peace and shared prosperity.

Building a World United by Kindness and Love

The vision of a world woven together by threads of kindness and love is not a utopian fantasy; it is a tangible future, achievable through the conscious and consistent practice of virtues that reside within each of us. This is the culmination of our exploration in this chapter – a call to recognize that the transformation of our societies begins not with grand, sweeping pronouncements or systemic overhauls alone, but with the quiet, potent power of individual actions, fueled by empathy, compassion, and a deep-seated respect for all life. When we cultivate these qualities within ourselves, we don't merely change our personal landscape; we become catalysts for a profound societal shift, radiating positivity that can touch and transform the lives of those around us, and ultimately, ripple outwards to encompass the globe.

Empathy, the profound ability to step into another's shoes and feel the world as they might, is the bedrock upon which a loving society is built. It allows us to move beyond our own immediate perspectives, to understand the joys and sorrows, the hopes and fears that shape the experiences of others. When we practice empathy, we naturally extend compassion. Compassion is empathy in action – the active desire to alleviate the suffering of others. It is this desire that compels us to offer a helping hand to a neighbor in need, to speak out against injustice, or simply to offer a listening ear to someone burdened by their troubles. Imagine the cumulative effect of billions of such acts, each one a small ember of warmth in the vast expanse of human interaction. These are the moments that begin to mend the fractures in our social fabric, replacing suspicion with trust and indifference with care.

Consider the simple, yet powerful, act of offering genuine respect. Respect, in its purest form, is the acknowledgment of the inherent worth and dignity of every individual, regardless of their background, beliefs, or circumstances. It means listening attentively when someone speaks, valuing their opinions even when they differ from our own, and treating them with courtesy and consideration in every interaction. When we extend respect, we create an environment where people feel seen, heard, and valued. This, in turn, fosters a sense of belonging and reduces the likelihood of conflict stemming from feelings of marginalization or disrespect. In workplaces, communities, and even within our own families, the consistent application of respect can dissolve tensions, encourage collaboration, and build bridges of understanding where walls of division once stood. It is the quiet affirmation that "you matter," a fundamental human need that, when met, unlocks potential and fosters positive engagement.

Furthermore, as we've discussed, contentment plays a crucial role in this grand mosaic of a loving society. When individuals are at peace with themselves and their circumstances, less driven by envy or the incessant need for more, they possess a greater capacity to give freely of themselves. Their generosity is not born out of obligation or a desire for recognition, but from a deep wellspring of inner satisfaction. A contented individual is less likely to hoard resources, whether material or emotional, and more inclined to share, to support, and to contribute to the well-being of the collective. This inner peace acts as a powerful buffer against the corrosive forces of greed and competition that so often undermine social harmony. It allows us to celebrate the successes of others without feeling diminished, and to approach challenges with a spirit of cooperation rather than rivalry.

The transformative power of kindness, when practiced consistently, is immense. Kindness is not merely about grand gestures; it is woven into the fabric of our daily lives through countless small actions. It's the smile offered to a stranger, the thoughtful word spoken to a colleague, the patient guidance given to a child. These acts, seemingly insignificant in isolation, accumulate to create a palpable atmosphere of warmth and positivity. They build resilience, not just for the recipient, but also for the giver. Studies have shown that acts of kindness can boost mood, reduce stress, and even improve physical health. When we are kind, we tap into our most authentic selves, nurturing our own well-being while simultaneously contributing to the well-being of others. This reciprocal relationship between giving and receiving kindness creates a virtuous cycle that can elevate entire communities.

Imagine a world where empathy is not an occasional act of deliberate effort, but a cultivated habit. A world where we instinctively seek to understand the perspectives of others before judging. This requires a conscious effort to listen more than we speak, to ask clarifying questions, and to suspend our own preconceived notions. It means recognizing that every individual carries a unique story, shaped by a complex interplay of experiences, influences, and internal landscapes. When we approach each interaction with this understanding, we create a space for genuine connection and mutual appreciation, dismantling the barriers of misunderstanding that so often lead to conflict. This empathetic approach allows us to see the shared humanity that binds us, transcending superficial differences and fostering a profound sense of interconnectedness.

Coupled with empathy is the unwavering commitment to compassion. Compassion moves us beyond understanding to a place of active caring.

It is the impulse to alleviate suffering, to offer comfort, and to stand in solidarity with those who are struggling. This can manifest in myriad ways, from donating to charitable causes and volunteering our time to offering emotional support to friends and family. In a broader societal context, compassion fuels advocacy for social justice, drives efforts to address poverty and inequality, and inspires innovation aimed at solving humanitarian crises. When compassion is a guiding principle, our policies and our social structures naturally begin to reflect a deeper care for the well-being of all members of society, especially the most vulnerable.

The practice of respect, as a cornerstone of our interactions, ensures that these acts of empathy and compassion are rooted in dignity. Respect is not conditional; it is a fundamental acknowledgment of each person's intrinsic value. This means treating everyone with courtesy, listening to their perspectives without interruption, and valuing their contributions, however small they may seem. In diverse societies, where differing opinions, beliefs, and lifestyles are commonplace, mutual respect becomes the essential glue that holds and bonds us together.

It allows for healthy debate and disagreement without devolving into animosity, fostering an environment where collective problem-solving can flourish. When we respect each other, we create a safe harbor for vulnerability and authenticity, allowing true relationships to form and strengthen.

Contentment, as the internal compass guiding our actions, ensures that our pursuit of progress and personal growth is not at the expense of others. It is the quiet understanding that true fulfillment comes from within, from meaningful connections, purposeful contribution, and inner peace, rather than from the endless accumulation of external validation or material possessions. When we are content, our motivations shift. We become less driven by comparison and competition, and more by a desire to contribute positively to the world around us. This inner alignment allows our acts of kindness and love to be pure, unadulterated by underlying insecurity or a need to prove our worth. It fosters a generosity of spirit that is essential for building a truly loving and supportive society.

Consider the profound impact of integrating these virtues into our daily routines. It means consciously choosing to respond with kindness rather than anger when faced with frustration. It means actively seeking to understand the viewpoint of someone with whom we disagree, rather than immediately dismissing it. It means recognizing the inherent dignity in every human being, from the CEO to the sanitation worker, and treating them accordingly. It means practicing gratitude for what we have, rather than fixating on what we lack, thereby freeing ourselves to give more freely. These are not extraordinary feats; they are the quiet, consistent choices that, when embraced collectively, have the power to reshape our world.

The ripple effect of such a shift is immeasurable. When individuals feel understood and respected, they are more likely to extend understanding and respect to others. When acts of kindness become commonplace, they create a culture where generosity and mutual support are the norm. When contentment replaces ceaseless striving, communities become more collaborative and less prone to division. This is how we build a world united by kindness and love – not by waiting for someone else to lead, but by becoming the leaders of our own lives, embodying the principles we wish to see reflected in society. Each one of us holds the potential to be a beacon of light, illuminating the path towards a more peaceful and loving global family.

Our individual journey towards embodying these virtues is a continuous process of learning and growth. It involves self-awareness, the willingness to examine our own biases and habits, and the courage to step outside our comfort zones. It is about embracing vulnerability, recognizing that it is in our moments of imperfection that we often connect most deeply with others. When we allow ourselves to be seen, flaws and all, we create the space for authentic connection, paving the way for genuine love and understanding to flourish. This journey is not always easy; it requires perseverance, forgiveness (both of ourselves and others), and an unwavering belief in the possibility of a better world.

The interconnectedness of all beings means that our individual choices have far-reaching consequences. An act of kindness, no matter how small, can create a positive cascade, influencing the mood and behavior of those who witness it. A moment of empathy can de-escalate a potential conflict and open the door to reconciliation. A commitment to respect can foster an environment where diverse perspectives are welcomed and valued, leading to richer solutions and stronger communities. By consciously choosing to infuse our lives with kindness, love, empathy, respect, and contentment, we actively participate in the creation of a society that reflects these most cherished human qualities. We become the architects of a future where peace and understanding are not distant aspirations, but lived realities for all.

Therefore, let this be our guiding principle as we move forward: to be intentional in our actions, mindful in our interactions, and unwavering in our commitment to fostering a world united by kindness and love. Let us be the change we wish to see, by embodying the virtues that can transform our communities and our planet. The path is illuminated by the light of our own compassionate hearts, and the journey, though challenging at times, is infinitely rewarding. By choosing love over fear, empathy over indifference, and kindness over judgment, we contribute to the unfolding of a truly magnificent human tapestry, woven with threads of connection, understanding, and an enduring, universal love. This is our shared legacy, our collective aspiration, and our greatest opportunity to build a world that truly reflects the best of what humanity can be.

Chapter 5: The Lasting Legacy of Mindful Living

True Greatness Beyond Material Wealth

The modern world often equates greatness with visible achievements – the colossal skyscraper, the record-breaking financial portfolio, the celebrity's global fame. These are the metrics by which success is frequently measured, external markers of power, influence, and material prosperity. Yet, if we pause to consider the legacies that truly resonate through time, the impact that genuinely transforms lives and elevates humanity, we discover a different kind of measure, one rooted not in acquisition but in essence, not in possession but in contribution, and not in outward display but in inward character.

This chapter delves into the nature of true greatness, a concept that transcends the ephemeral allure of material wealth and societal status to embrace the enduring power of mindful living and its profound impact on our world.

True greatness, fundamentally, is not about the accumulation of possessions or the attainment of high-status positions. It is about the cultivation of virtues that enrich both the individual and the collective. It is found in the consistent practice of empathy, the ability to truly understand and share the feelings of another. It is present in compassion, the active desire to alleviate suffering and promote well-being. It resides in integrity, the unwavering commitment to ethical principles and authenticity, even when no one is watching. These are the qualities that, when embodied, create ripples of positive change that extend far beyond our immediate sphere of influence. Consider the countless individuals throughout history whose names may not be emblazoned on public monuments or economic reports, yet whose quiet acts of kindness, courage, and wisdom have profoundly shaped the course of human events. These are the unsung heroes whose greatness lies not in what they owned, but in what they gave, in how they lived, and in the indelible mark they left on the human spirit.

The pursuit of material wealth, while a natural human endeavor to secure comfort and opportunity, can become a gilded cage when it is mistaken for the pinnacle of achievement. When our lives become solely oriented towards the accumulation of more – more money, more possessions, more status – we risk losing sight of what truly nourishes the soul and contributes to a meaningful existence. The transient satisfaction derived from acquiring an object or reaching a financial milestone often fades, leaving us in search of the next acquisition, perpetuating a cycle of never-ending desire. This constant striving for external validation can erode our inner peace, creating anxiety and a sense of emptiness. True greatness, conversely, stems from an internal source of fulfillment. It arises from a deep wellspring of self-acceptance, purpose, and connection, qualities that cannot be bought or earned through financial transactions. When we shift our focus from what we can acquire to what we can contribute, from accumulating wealth to cultivating wisdom and compassion, we unlock a far more profound and enduring form of success.

Think of the individuals who, despite modest financial circumstances, have lived lives of immense impact. The teacher who ignores low pay for the reward of shaping young minds, instilling in them a lifelong love of learning and critical thinking. The caregiver who dedicates their life to tending to the sick and elderly, offering comfort, dignity, and unwavering support during their most vulnerable moments. The artist or musician whose creations bring beauty, solace, and inspiration to millions, often struggling to make ends meet but driven by an irrepressible creative impulse. These are individuals whose greatness is not measured by their bank balance, but by the depth of their commitment, the quality of their character, and the positive legacy they leave behind. Their lives are a testament to the fact that true value is not inherent in the material possessions one holds, but in the character, one cultivates, and the service one provides.

Furthermore, the notion of legacy itself is often misunderstood. We tend to think of legacy in terms of grand achievements, the enduring impact of one's work or influence on a large scale. While these are certainly aspects of legacy, the most potent and lasting legacies are often woven into the fabric of everyday life, transmitted through the values we embody and the relationships we nurture. A parent who instills in their children a strong sense of empathy and integrity leaves a legacy that will far outlast any financial inheritance. A friend who offers unwavering support during times of crisis creates a legacy of loyalty and care that can profoundly shape another person's life trajectory. These acts of personal connection, of love, kindness, and unwavering support, are the true building blocks of a meaningful legacy. They are the invisible threads that strengthen the human community, creating a tapestry of interconnected lives richer and more enduring than any material fortune.

Recognizing this distinction is crucial for cultivating a life of purpose and fulfillment. It encourages us to look inward, to identify our unique strengths and passions, and to find ways to express them in service to something larger than ourselves. It means understanding that our inherent worth is not tied to our economic status or our public recognition. We all possess the capacity for great impact, regardless of our financial standing. The potential for positive influence resides within each of us, waiting to be awakened through mindful intention and consistent action. This is not about achieving fame or fortune, but about living a life aligned with our deepest values, contributing our unique gifts to the world, and leaving it a little brighter than we found it.

The societal pressure to equate wealth with success can be relentless. We are bombarded with images of opulence and constant narratives that suggest happiness and fulfillment are directly proportional to our material possessions. This often leads to a corrosive form of comparison, where we measure our own lives against the perceived successes of others, fostering feelings of inadequacy or envy. However, when we consciously choose to redefine greatness, we liberate ourselves from this potentially damaging cycle. We begin to recognize that true prosperity is multifaceted, encompassing not only financial security but also emotional well-being, meaningful relationships, personal growth, and a sense of purpose.

A life rich in these qualities, even without immense material wealth, is a life of true abundance.

Consider the example of individuals who have dedicated their lives to humanitarian causes or social justice movements, often operating with limited resources but driven by an unshakeable moral compass. Their impact is measured not in dollars earned, but in lives touched, injustices challenged, and positive change enacted. Their courage, their perseverance, and their unwavering belief in a better world are the hallmarks of their greatness. They demonstrate that the most profound contributions to humanity often arise from a place of deep conviction and a willingness to sacrifice personal comfort for a greater good. Their lives serve as a powerful reminder that true wealth lies in our capacity to make a difference, to uplift others, and to leave a positive imprint on the world.

This shift in perspective also fosters a greater sense of contentment. When we are not perpetually chasing external validation through material accumulation, we can begin to appreciate what we already have. Gratitude becomes a more prominent force in our lives, allowing us to find joy in simple pleasures and to recognize the abundance that already surrounds us. Contentment, in this context, is not complacency; it is a profound appreciation for the present moment and a deep understanding that fulfillment is an inside job.

It frees us from the anxiety of scarcity and the endless pursuit of "more," allowing us to engage more fully with life and to contribute more generously from a place of inner peace.

The essence of true greatness, therefore, lies in the cultivation of character and the commitment to making a positive contribution, however small, to the world. It is about recognizing that the most valuable assets we possess are our integrity, our compassion, our ability to connect with others, and our capacity for growth. These are the qualities that, when nurtured, lead to lives of profound meaning and lasting impact.

They are the foundations upon which a truly rich and fulfilling existence is built, a legacy that extends far beyond the material realm and resonates through the hearts and minds of generations to come. By embracing this understanding, we can redefine success on our own terms, pursuing a path of contribution and character that leads to a truly great life, measured not by accumulation, but by impact and by the enduring light we bring to the world.

Embracing Empathy – Our Shared Responsibility

Empathy, at its core, is the profound capacity to step into another's shoes, to feel with them, and to understand their world from their perspective.

It is the gentle thread that weaves through the tapestry of human connection, binding us together in a shared experience of existence. While we often speak of it as an individual virtue, it is crucial to recognize empathy as a collective endeavor, a shared responsibility that falls upon each member of our global family. Our ability to truly connect with one another, to foster understanding across differences, and to build a society that thrives on mutual respect and support hinges on our collective embrace of this fundamental human quality.

Cultivating empathy is not merely an act of personal betterment; it is an essential practice that profoundly enriches our individual lives. When we extend ourselves to understand another's feelings, we open ourselves to a wider spectrum of human experience. This process broadens our own emotional intelligence, allowing us to navigate complex social landscapes with greater nuance and wisdom. It helps us to move beyond our own immediate concerns and to see the world through a more expansive lens, fostering a deeper appreciation for the diversity of human thought and emotion. By actively practicing empathy, we not only offer solace and support to others but also unlock a richer, more meaningful inner life for ourselves, marked by a heightened sense of connection and belonging.

Beyond the personal sphere, the active cultivation and expression of empathy serves as the bedrock upon which a strong and resilient society is built. It is the silent architect of understanding in our daily interactions, the quiet force that mends the inevitable fractures that arise in human relationships. When we approach conversations with a genuine desire to comprehend the other person's viewpoint, even when it diverges significantly from our own, we create an atmosphere of trust and openness. This empathetic listening, devoid of judgment and defensiveness, is the first step in effective communication. It allows for the honest exchange of ideas, fostering clarity and preventing misunderstandings that can escalate into conflict. Without this foundational element of empathy, communication becomes a series of monologues, each person speaking past the other, rather than a collaborative dance of shared meaning.

Moreover, empathy is an indispensable tool for conflict resolution. Disputes, whether personal, professional, or societal, often stem from a lack of understanding or an inability to acknowledge the validity of another's feelings or experiences. By consciously choosing to empathize, we can de-escalate tensions and find common ground. When individuals feel heard and understood, even in disagreement, they are more likely to engage constructively in finding solutions. This doesn't mean agreeing with the other person's perspective, but rather acknowledging its existence and the emotional weight it carries for them. This is particularly vital in a world marked by increasing polarization and division. Empathetic engagement offers a pathway towards reconciliation, helping to bridge divides and rebuild fractured relationships, fostering a sense of shared humanity even amidst profound differences.

The power of empathy to build bridges across diverse communities cannot be overstated. Our globalized world is a vibrant mosaic of cultures, beliefs, and lived experiences. It is precisely in this rich diversity that the greatest potential for misunderstanding and conflict lies. However, it is also within this diversity that the most profound opportunities for connection and growth emerge, opportunities that are unlocked by empathy. When we make a conscious effort to understand the histories, values, and aspirations of people from different backgrounds, we dismantle the barriers of prejudice and ignorance. This empathetic curiosity encourages dialogue, breaks down stereotypes, and fosters genuine appreciation for the richness that diversity brings. It transforms abstract notions of tolerance into tangible acts of connection, creating communities where individuals feel seen, valued, and respected for who they are.

Consider the impact of empathy in our everyday interactions. It's in the way a doctor listens attentively to a patient's concerns, not just for the physical symptoms but for the underlying anxieties and fears. It's in the way a teacher recognizes the unique learning style and emotional needs of each student, tailoring their approach to foster growth and confidence. It's in the way a friend offers a listening ear and a comforting presence to someone going through a difficult time, without judgment or the need to offer unsolicited advice. These are not grand, public gestures, but quiet, consistent acts of empathetic connection that form the very fabric of our social bonds. They are the micro-interactions that, when multiplied across communities, create a ripple effect of goodwill and understanding.

Furthermore, empathy acts as a powerful catalyst for positive social change. Movements that have sought to address injustice and inequality have almost invariably been fueled by a profound sense of empathy for those who are marginalized or suffering. When individuals and groups feel the pain of others as if it were their own, they are moved to action. This compassionate drive, born from empathetic understanding, can inspire collective efforts to challenge oppressive systems, advocate for the vulnerable, and create a more just and equitable world. It transforms passive observation into active engagement, empowering individuals to contribute to solutions and to work towards a common good. The history of social progress is replete with examples of individuals who, driven by empathy, have dared to challenge the status quo and to create a lasting positive change for the better.

It is crucial to reframe our understanding of empathy, moving it from the periphery of optional personal traits to the very center of essential human connection. Empathy is not a passive feeling; it is an active choice, a commitment to engage with the world from a place of understanding and compassion. It requires conscious effort to set aside our own biases, to listen deeply, and to consider perspectives that may be unfamiliar or even uncomfortable. This active engagement is what truly cultivates a more connected and harmonious existence, both for ourselves and for the wider world.

The practice of empathy is a continuous journey, not a destination. There will be times when it is challenging, when our own experiences or beliefs create a natural resistance to understanding another's perspective. In these moments, it is important to understand and remember that empathy does not equate to endorsement or agreement. It is about recognizing the shared humanity that binds us, even in the face of profound disagreement.

It is about acknowledging the validity of another person's lived reality and the emotions that accompany it. This willingness to engage with difficult perspectives, to practice empathetic curiosity, is what allows us to grow as individuals and to strengthen the bonds of our collective human family.

To truly embrace empathy as a shared responsibility, we must actively cultivate it in our daily lives. This can begin with simple practices, such as mindful listening in conversations, consciously trying to understand the unspoken emotions behind someone's words, and seeking out diverse perspectives through literature, film, and genuine interaction. It involves asking ourselves: "How might this person be feeling?" or "What experiences might have led them to this belief?" These small, deliberate acts of intentionality can profoundly shift our orientation towards others, fostering a more compassionate and connected way of being in the world.

The ripple effect of an empathetic society is transformative. When individuals feel genuinely understood and supported, they are more likely to extend that same grace to others. This creates a virtuous cycle of kindness and cooperation, where empathy becomes the prevailing ethos. Such a society is better equipped to tackle complex challenges, from environmental sustainability to global health crises, because its members are more inclined to collaborate and to prioritize the collective well-being.

It is a society where differences are celebrated, not feared, and where mutual respect forms the foundation for progress and shared prosperity.

Ultimately, our legacy, in its truest sense, is not measured by what we accumulate, but by the quality of our connections and the positive impact we have on the lives of others. Embracing empathy is central to building that legacy. It is the active embodiment of our shared humanity, a commitment to understanding, to compassion, and to the betterment of our collective existence. By choosing to cultivate and express empathy in all our interactions, we not only enrich our own lives but also contribute to a more connected, resilient, and harmonious world, leaving behind a legacy of genuine human connection that resonates far beyond our individual lifetimes. It is through this shared responsibility that we truly uphold the lasting legacy of mindful living.

The Intergenerational Impact of Kindness

The echoes of our actions, particularly those rooted in kindness, resonate far beyond our immediate present, weaving a complex and enduring narrative through the tapestry of generations. When we speak of mindful living, we are not merely contemplating our individual journey through this life but also considering the profound imprints we leave upon those who will follow.

The subtle, yet powerful, transmission of values, behaviors, and even financial wisdom across familial and community lines forms an intergenerational impact, shaping the very fabric of future societies. This is not a hypothetical construct; it is a tangible reality observable in the enduring legacies of families and communities that have prioritized the cultivation of thoughtful, considerate, and generous principles.

Consider, for instance, the seemingly small, everyday acts of kindness that become ingrained habits. A parent who consistently offers a helping hand to a neighbor, not out of obligation but out of genuine concern, is not just performing a singular act of goodwill. They are modeling a way of being, demonstrating that community support and mutual aid are not mere ideals but practical, lived realities. The child who witnesses this consistent behavior absorbs this lesson not through explicit instruction, but through observation and lived experience. This absorption becomes part of their own behavioral repertoire, influencing their interactions with peers, their future family, and their wider community. Over time, this internalized habit of kindness can cascade, creating a generational predisposition towards helpfulness and social responsibility. Imagine a family where, for generations, there has been a tradition of volunteering at local shelters, or of checking in on elderly relatives and neighbors. This isn't accidental; it's the product of a deliberate, albeit often unconscious, passing down of values. Each generation learns, by example and by participation, that contributing to the well-being of others is an integral part of a fulfilling life. This creates a powerful, positive feedback loop, where acts of kindness become not the exception, but the norm, shaping the character of individuals and the ethos of the communities they inhabit.

Beyond the realm of purely altruistic acts, the transmission of financial wisdom also plays a significant role in this intergenerational legacy. A parent who teaches their child the importance of saving, of living within one's means, and of responsible stewardship of resources is imparting a legacy of financial prudence. This isn't just about accumulating wealth; it's about fostering a mindset of security, foresight, and the ability to weather life's inevitable storms. When children grow up understanding the value of a dollar, the dangers of unchecked debt, and the satisfaction of delayed gratification, they are better equipped to build stable lives for themselves and their own families. This financial literacy, passed down through conversations, shared budgeting practices, and modeling responsible spending, can create a generational advantage, lifting families out of cycles of poverty and towards greater economic security. Conversely, a lack of such instruction can perpetuate financial struggles across generations, creating a burden that is difficult to overcome. Therefore, teaching children about money management is an act of profound intergenerational kindness, providing them with the tools and knowledge necessary for a more secure future that's ahead.

The way we conduct ourselves, our general demeanor and respectful conduct, also leaves an indelible mark. A grandparent who always greets strangers with a warm smile and a polite word, who listens attentively when others speak, and who approaches disagreements with a calm and rational demeanor, is demonstrating a form of social grace that can be deeply influential. This emphasis on respect for oneself and for others becomes a foundational element of character. Children who witness this consistent respect learn to value courtesy, to engage in civil discourse, and to treat everyone with a baseline level of dignity. This translates into more harmonious relationships, fewer interpersonal conflicts, and a stronger sense of social cohesion. Think of a community where such respectful interactions are common. It fosters an environment where people feel safer, more connected, and more willing to engage with one another constructively. This isn't an accident of nature; it's the cultivated outcome of generations of individuals choosing to live mindfully and to treat others with consideration.

Consider the historical examples that illustrate this principle. Many immigrant families, arriving in new lands with little more than the clothes on their backs, managed to build prosperous lives for their descendants through a combination of hard work, frugality, and a strong emphasis on education and respect. These were not individuals who benefited from inherited wealth or privilege, but rather those who possessed an internalized set of values that prioritized long-term gain over immediate gratification, and community well-being over individualistic pursuits. They instilled in their children a sense of duty, a commitment to excellence, and a deep appreciation for the opportunities they were afforded. This dedication to passing on these core principles, often through storytelling, shared labor, and the establishment of community institutions, created a powerful engine for upward mobility and generational success. The kindness shown in sharing scarce resources, the financial discipline in saving for future ventures, and the respectful interactions within their own communities all contributed to a legacy that extended far beyond their own lifetimes.

The impact of kindness can also be seen in the way families approach challenges. A family that faces adversity, such as illness or financial hardship, with resilience and mutual support, is teaching a profound lesson about inner strength. When parents, in the face of difficulty, prioritize the emotional well-being of their children, offer words of encouragement, and work together to find solutions, they are imbuing their offspring with a powerful sense of hope and agency. This learned resilience becomes a valuable inheritance, enabling future generations to navigate their own difficulties with greater fortitude. It's the opposite of a family where hardship leads to despair, blame, or fragmentation. In those instances, the negative impact can also be transmitted, creating cycles of emotional distress and instability. The mindful choice to respond to adversity with grace and solidarity, however, creates a legacy of inner strength that is perhaps the most precious gift one can bestow.

Furthermore, the mindful cultivation of gratitude within a family or community can have a transformative intergenerational effect. When individuals are regularly encouraged to acknowledge and appreciate the good things in their lives, no matter how small, they develop a more positive outlook. This practice of gratitude, passed down through shared expressions of thankfulness, journaling, or simply verbalizing appreciation, fosters contentment and reduces feelings of envy or dissatisfaction. Children who grow up in an atmosphere of gratitude are more likely to be happy, to experience less stress, and to have more fulfilling relationships. They learn to see abundance where others might see scarcity, and to celebrate what they have rather than lamenting what they lack. This optimistic perspective, nurtured over generations, can create a powerful societal advantage, fostering communities that are more joyful, supportive, and less prone to the negative consequences of consumerism and comparison.

The simple act of sharing knowledge and skills is another powerful form of intergenerational kindness. A grandparent who teaches a grandchild how to garden, how to cook a family recipe, or how to play a musical instrument is not just imparting practical abilities. They are also sharing a piece of their history, their culture, and their passion. These shared experiences create bonds, foster a sense of belonging, and provide individuals with a connection to their heritage. This transmission of knowledge ensures that traditions are kept alive, that skills are not lost, and that the richness of human experience is passed from one generation to the next. When this sharing is done with patience, encouragement, and a genuine desire to see the learner succeed, it becomes an act of profound kindness, enriching lives and preserving cultural identity for the future.

It is also important to consider the impact of conscious decision-making regarding ethical conduct. When parents instill in their children a strong moral compass, emphasizing honesty, integrity, and fairness, they are laying the groundwork for future generations of principled individuals. This commitment to ethical behavior, demonstrated through consistent actions and open discussions about moral dilemmas, shapes the character of individuals and, by extension, the ethical standards of society. Imagine a business founded on principles of fair trade and customer service, where these values have been rigorously upheld and passed down through successive generations of leadership. Such a legacy not only ensures the longevity of the enterprise but also contributes positively to the economic and social landscape in which it operates. It demonstrates that profitability and ethical conduct are not mutually exclusive but rather can be mutually reinforcing.

The ripple effect of kindness, financial prudence, and respectful conduct is not always immediate or dramatic. Often, its power lies in its subtlety and persistence. It is the quiet strength that underpins stable families, resilient communities, and flourishing societies. Each act of mindful living, each deliberate choice to act with consideration for others, contributes to this ongoing legacy. It is a continuous process of sowing seeds that will blossom in the lives of those who come after us.

To truly embrace this intergenerational impact, we must become more conscious of the messages we are sending, both through our words and, more importantly, through our actions. Are we modeling the behavior we wish to see in future generations? Are we nurturing kindness, teaching financial responsibility, and demonstrating respect in our daily interactions? These are not abstract philosophical questions, but practical considerations that have tangible consequences for the future. The legacy we leave is not solely determined by our material possessions or grand achievements, but by the quality of the human connections we foster and the enduring values we transmit.

The mindful practice of passing on these positive traits is a profound expression of love and responsibility. It is an acknowledgment that we are part of a continuum, a long chain of human experience, and that our actions today will shape the lives of those who are yet to be born. By consciously choosing to cultivate kindness, to impart financial wisdom, and to conduct ourselves with respect, we are not just living mindfully in the present; we are actively building a better future, one generation at a time. This conscious effort to imbue our lives with these enduring values is perhaps the most powerful and lasting legacy we can hope to create, a testament to the enduring power of mindful living to shape the world for the better, long after we are gone. It is in understanding this profound intergenerational connection that the true depth and significance of our present actions are revealed, urging us towards a more intentional and impactful way of being in the world. This ongoing transmission of positive attributes forms the bedrock of a sustainable and compassionate society, a living testament to the enduring power of human connection and the mindful cultivation of virtue.

Contentment as a Foundation for Peace

The pursuit of peace, both within ourselves and in the wider world, is an aspiration deeply woven into the human spirit. While external factors often dominate discussions of global harmony, the foundational element for achieving this cherished state lies not in grand political gestures or societal restructuring alone, but in the quiet, yet profound, cultivation of inner contentment. This subsection delves into the critical role that personal satisfaction plays in forging a more peaceful existence, exploring how a state of grateful acceptance can act as an antidote to the corrosive influences that breed conflict and discord.

At its core, contentment is the quiet appreciation of what is, rather than a restless yearning for what is not. It is the gentle recognition of abundance in the present moment, a stark contrast to the insatiable craving that often fuels dissatisfaction. When individuals are genuinely content, they are less driven by the need to acquire more, to outperform others, or to constantly seek external validation. This internal equilibrium naturally reduces the seeds of envy and greed, two powerful drivers of conflict at both personal and societal levels. Consider the individual who finds joy in a simple meal, a warm conversation, or the beauty of a sunset. Their sense of fulfillment is derived from an internal source, making them less susceptible to the competitive pressures that can lead to resentment and animosity. This intrinsic satisfaction acts as a buffer, protecting them from the pervasive feeling of "not enough" that can permeate modern life and push individuals towards actions that disrupt peace.

Gratitude serves as the cornerstone of this contentment. When we cultivate a practice of acknowledging and appreciating the blessings in our lives, however modest, we shift our focus from perceived deficiencies to existing abundance. This intentional redirection of attention has a profound impact on our emotional landscape. Instead of dwelling on what we lack, we begin to recognize the richness that is already present. This practice is not about passive acceptance of unfavorable circumstances, but rather about acknowledging the positive aspects of our reality, even amidst challenges. A person who is grateful for their health, for supportive relationships, or for the opportunity to learn, even while navigating difficult times, is cultivating a resilient inner peace. This gratitude, when practiced consistently, reshapes our perception, transforming our internal environment into one that fosters tranquility rather than turmoil. It truly creates a fertile ground for peace to flourish, as the very inclination to envy or resent diminishes.

Living within one's means is an extension of this principle of contentment. It is the practical embodiment of appreciating what one has and making responsible choices based on that appreciation. In a consumer-driven society, the pressure to accumulate possessions and maintain a certain lifestyle can be immense. However, when individuals are grounded in contentment, they are more likely to make choices that align with their true needs and values, rather than succumbing to external pressures or the illusion of happiness through acquisition. This mindful approach to finances—saving diligently, spending responsibly, and avoiding unnecessary debt—not only fosters personal security but also contributes to a more stable societal environment. Economies built on excessive consumption and debt are inherently fragile and prone to disruptions that can have far-reaching consequences.

Conversely, a population that embraces financial prudence, born out of contentment, creates a more resilient and sustainable economic fabric, reducing the potential for widespread financial distress that can ignite social unrest.

The ripple effect of individual contentment on societal peace is undeniable. When a significant portion of the population operates from a place of inner peace and gratitude, the collective atmosphere shifts. Divisive forces such as envy, greed, and dissatisfaction lose their potency. The constant striving and comparison that often characterize social interactions begin to wane, replaced by a greater sense of community and mutual respect. Imagine a society where people are genuinely happy with their circumstances, where they celebrate the successes of others without feeling diminished, and where their interactions are guided by a spirit of generosity rather than competition. Such a society would naturally be more peaceful, more cooperative, and more resilient in the face of adversity. The collective energy would be directed towards constructive endeavors rather than destructive rivalries.

This personal pathway to peace is not an abdication of responsibility or an endorsement of complacency. Rather, it is a strategic redirection of energy and focus. By cultivating inner contentment, we are not ignoring the world's problems, but we are equipping ourselves with the internal resources to address them from a place of strength and clarity. A person who is at peace with themselves is better equipped to act with compassion, to engage in constructive dialogue, and to contribute to solutions without being driven by anger, frustration, or a sense of personal lack. This inner peace acts as a powerful foundation for meaningful action in the world. It allows us to engage with others authentically, to offer support without expectation of reward, and to contribute to the collective good from a place of overflow rather than deficit.

The practice of mindful living, as discussed throughout this book, directly nurtures this essential contentment. By paying attention to our thoughts, emotions, and surroundings without judgment, we become more aware of the patterns that lead to dissatisfaction. We learn to identify the triggers for envy, the allure of external validation, and the endless cycle of wanting more. Through mindfulness, we can gently interrupt these patterns, choosing instead to focus on the present moment, to practice gratitude, and to appreciate the simple gifts of existence. This ongoing cultivation of mindfulness becomes a virtuous cycle, where greater awareness leads to greater contentment, which in turn fosters a deeper sense of peace.

Ultimately, embracing contentment as a personal pathway to peace is an act of profound love—love for oneself, love for others, and love for the world. It is a recognition that the most sustainable and enduring peace begins within. When we are content, we are more likely to extend kindness, to practice forgiveness, and to engage with the world from a place of abundance and generosity. This creates a positive ripple effect, transforming not only our own lives but also the lives of those around us, and contributing to a more tranquil and loving world for all. It is in this quiet cultivation of inner satisfaction that the seeds of a truly peaceful existence are sown, promising a harvest of harmony for generations to come. The legacy of mindful living, therefore, is intrinsically linked to the legacy of peace, a legacy built not on the absence of conflict, but on the presence of profound, unshakeable contentment within the human heart.

Leaving a Legacy of Love and Respect

The tapestry of a life lived mindfully is not solely woven from moments of personal tranquility, but also from the enduring threads of the impact we have on others. As we near the culmination of our exploration into mindful living, it is natural to turn our gaze outward, contemplating the legacy we are actively creating. This is not merely about the tangible accomplishments that might appear on a resume or be etched in stone, but about the subtler, yet infinitely more profound, imprint we leave on the hearts and minds of those whose lives we touch. The most resonant and lasting legacies are often forged not in grand gestures or extraordinary feats, but in the consistent, unwavering practice of love and respect in our everyday interactions.

Consider the profound influence of kindness. It is a currency that never depreciates, a gift that returns to the giver multiplied. A simple word of encouragement, a patient ear offered in a moment of distress, a helping hand extended without expectation – these are the building blocks of a legacy of love. They are the quiet echoes that continue to resonate long after the spoken words have faded. Think of individuals who have inspired you most deeply. More often than not, it is not their accolades or their material wealth that comes to mind, but the way they made you feel – seen, valued, and respected. This inherent human need for connection and validation is the fertile ground upon which a legacy of love is built. By consistently choosing empathy over judgment, compassion over indifference, and understanding over condemnation, we cultivate an environment where trust and genuine connection can flourish. This creates a positive ripple effect, influencing not only our immediate circle but extending outward in ways we may never fully comprehend.

Respect, too, is a cornerstone of a life that leaves a meaningful imprint. It is the acknowledgement of the inherent worth and dignity of every individual, regardless of their background, beliefs, or circumstances. This means actively listening, valuing diverse perspectives, and refraining from imposing our own views or prejudices. When we approach others with genuine respect, we create a space where authentic dialogue can occur, fostering understanding and bridging divides. It's about recognizing that everyone is on their own journey, facing their own unique challenges and possessing their own invaluable insights. In a world that can often feel polarized and contentious, the deliberate practice of respectful engagement can be a powerful force for healing and connection. It's in the willingness to see the humanity in another, even when we disagree, that we truly honor the spirit of mindful living and build a legacy that transcends superficial differences.

Living authentically is intrinsically linked to leaving a legacy of love and respect. When we are true to ourselves, our values, and our convictions, we radiate an integrity that is deeply compelling. This authenticity allows us to connect with others on a deeper level, as it demonstrates a courage to be vulnerable and transparent. It means aligning our actions with our innermost beliefs, even when it's difficult or unpopular. This unwavering commitment to one's truth, expressed with grace and consideration for others, builds trust and inspires genuine admiration. It signals to the world that we are not easily swayed by external pressures or the desire for superficial approval, but are guided by a deeper, more meaningful compass. This inner steadfastness creates a stable presence, a reliable anchor in an often-unpredictable world, leaving a legacy of strength and conviction.

The principle of financial prudence, explored earlier in the context of contentment, also plays a crucial role in the legacy we leave. It is not about the accumulation of wealth for its own sake, but about the responsible stewardship of resources. By practicing mindful spending, saving diligently, and avoiding unnecessary debt, we not only secure our own future but also demonstrate a commitment to responsibility and foresight. This can translate into a legacy of stability for our families, the ability to support causes we believe in, and the freedom to act with generosity when opportunities arise. Financial integrity is a testament to our character, showing that we can manage our affairs with wisdom and discipline. This practical aspect of mindful living contributes to a legacy of reliability and enables us to be more effective in supporting those around us and contributing to the well-being of our communities.

Ultimately, the legacy we leave is a reflection of the values we have consistently embodied. It is the sum total of our choices, our actions, and our intentions. By consciously cultivating inner contentment, practicing financial prudence, living authentically, and extending love and respect to all we encounter, we are actively weaving a tapestry of a life well-lived. This is not about achieving perfection, but about a dedicated, ongoing effort to live in alignment with our highest ideals. The impact of such a life is immeasurable. It extends beyond our own existence, shaping the perspectives and experiences of future generations. It serves as a quiet testament to the power of mindful living, demonstrating that true fulfillment and lasting significance are found not in grand pronouncements, but in the consistent, heartfelt practice of simple, profound human virtues. Each act of kindness, each moment of genuine respect, each authentic expression of self, contributes to a legacy that truly matters, resonating with the enduring values that define our shared humanity. This is the enduring power of a life lived with intention and heart, a legacy of love and respect that continues to blossom long after we are gone.

ACKNOWLEDGMENTS

This journey of mindful living, culminating in this exploration of our legacy, would not have been possible without the quiet strength and unwavering support of many. I also extend my deepest thanks to my mentors, whose wisdom and guidance have shaped my perspective and encouraged me to delve deeper into the profound impact of our actions. To the countless individuals who have shared their stories, their struggles, and their triumphs, you have enriched this work immeasurably, offering the raw, beautiful truth of human experience. And to you, the reader, thank you for embarking on this exploration; may the insights gained here empower you to weave a legacy of love and respect that resonates through your life and beyond.

APPENDIX

The principles outlined in this book are rooted in practices that can be further explored and deepened. For those seeking to cultivate a more profound sense of mindful living and legacy creation, the following resources are recommended:

Our Worlds Apart: A fascinating romance book by Dr. *A*. Romani.
Unlocking Your All: A self-help book by Dr. *A*. Romani that guides you on everyday life, work and social skills you'll want to know.
Viewing Food Through the Lens of Nourishment: A Comprehensive Guide to Mastering Healthy Cooking: Nutritional basics, cookbook, meal planning, and much more by Dr. *A*. Romani.

These resources are designed to be living tools, evolving with your personal growth and offering continued support as you consciously craft a life of meaning and enduring positive influence.

Visit any of the below sites to learn more.

www.AuthoredPages.com
www.InkprintPublishingHouse.com
www.LeafyPen.com
www.PinionBook.com

GLOSSARY

Authenticity: The quality of being genuine and true to one's own personality, spirit, or character, aligning actions with inner values and beliefs.

Contentment: A state of inner peace and satisfaction with what one has, rather than a constant striving for more.

Empathy: The ability to understand and share the feelings of another.

Financial Prudence: The practice of careful and responsible management of financial resources, emphasizing foresight and avoiding unnecessary debt.

Legacy: The lasting impact or imprint an individual leaves on the world, often through their actions, values, and the influence they have on others.

Mindful Living: A state of active, open attention to the present, acknowledging one's thoughts, feelings, and surroundings without judgment.

Respect: A feeling of deep admiration for someone or something elicited by their abilities, qualities, or achievements; or the due regard for the feelings, wishes, rights, or traditions of others.

Stewardship: The responsible overseeing and protection of something considered worth caring for and preserving.

REFERENCES

1. **Romani, Dr. A. (2025).** *Our Worlds Apart.* Pinion Books.

2. **Romani, Dr. A. (2025).** *Unlocking Your All.* Authored Pages.

3. **Romani, Dr. A. (2025).** *Viewing Food Through the Lens of Nourishment.* Leafy Pen.

BIOGRAPHY

Dr. A. Romani is an indie author and inspirational storyteller who's made waves in the literary world with his unique voice and compelling narratives. Armed with a doctorate that sharpened his research and communication skills, he's built a diverse portfolio spanning multiple genres—each infused with his signature blend of inspiration and insight. What sets **Dr. Romani** apart is his commitment to the transformative power of stories. He doesn't just put books out there; he creates movements of positivity and encouragement. Through his Indie Author works, he connects directly with readers seeking both entertainment and enlightenment. His books consistently resonate with audiences worldwide, offering comfort and motivation to those navigating their own life stories. **Dr. Romani** believes every story has the potential to change lives, and he's dedicated to being that beacon of hope— one book, one story at a time.